# A
# Kingdom of Priests:
## Liturgical Formation
## of the People of God

Papers read at the International Anglican Liturgical Consultation
Brixen, North Italy, 24-25 August 1987

## edited by Thomas J. Talley

*Professor of Liturgics, General Theological Seminary, New York*

## THE ALCUIN CLUB and the GROUP FOR RENEWAL OF WORSHIP (GROW)

The Alcuin Club, which exists to promote the study of Christian liturgy in general and of Anglican liturgy in particular, traditionally published a single volume annually for its members. This ceased in 1986. Similarly, GROW was responsible from 1975 to 1986 for the quarterly 'Grove Liturgical studies'. Since the beginning of 1987 the two have sponsored a Joint Editorial Board to produce quarterly 'Joint Liturgical Studies'. Full details of the separate organizations and of their respective previous publications are available. Details of the current series of Joint Liturgical Studies are available from Grove Books.

### THE COVER PICTURE
is designed to show the people of God active in worship

*First Impression* March 1988
**ISSN** 0951–2667
**ISBN** 1 85174 075 9

GROVE  BOOKS  LIMITED
Bramcote    Nottingham    NG9 3DS

# CONTENTS

## THE CONTRIBUTORS

David Holeton is Professor of Liturgics at Trinity College, Toronto, and a member of the Doctrine and Worship Committee of the Anglican Church in Canada (and Secretary of the Brixen Consultation)

Robert Brooks is a parish clergyman in Washington, D.C., and a member of the Standing Liturgical Commission of the Episcopal Church in the USA

Bryan Spinks is Chaplain of Churchill College Chapel, Cambridge, and a member of the Church of England Liturgical Commission

Daphne Fraser is a retired laywoman, once Secretary of the Church of England Liturgical Commission

Paul Gibson is Liturgical Officer of the Anglican Church in Canada

Elisha Mbonigaba is Lecturer in Worship at Bishop Tucker Theological College, Mukono, Uganda

Donald Gray is Canon Residentiary of Westminster Abbey, London (and Chairman of the Brixen Consultation)

# Introduction

## by the Editor

It is commonplace that our century has seen an explosion of liturgical development in all of western Christianity, development encouraged by our extended knowledge of the worship of the early Church and by appreciation of the understanding of the Church as the Body of Christ that breathes in those early documents. This development has been welcome, but with it have come new questions regarding the maintenance of liturgical identity, responsible formation of Christians as those who share in the priesthood of Christ, and the impact of that sharing on our understanding of the shape of the liturgical community.

Sixteen liturgical scholars of the Anglican Communion met together in Brixen (Bressanone) in northern Italy over two days, 24-25 August 1987, at the conclusion of the 1987 Congress of *Societas Liturgica* to discuss the formative role of the liturgy in the life of the People of God, under the theme, 'Liturgical Formation and Education'.

This consultation, assembled at the suggestion of the Anglican Consultative Council, was addressed by the Archbishop of Canterbury in a letter. He said,
'Historically, the Anglican Church has found identity and coherence in its liturgy. Thus when questions are arising about our identity today there is urgent need for such a Consultation as yours. Liturgy both mirrors and shapes a Church, and Anglicans can learn much about each other through studying how our shared liturgical heritage is being applied and developed in different provinces.'
That connection between the Church's worship and her identity is fundamental to any liturgical theology. Worship is the Church's constitutive activity.

On the other hand, if the Church's identity is to be organic rather than merely organizational, her forms of worship must reflect the local and historical circumstances of the actually assembled People of God. Those whose concern it is to study the historical development of liturgical forms know that the tension between continuity of tradition and contemporary and local relevance is a constant one in all the history of worship, and a 'changeless tradition' is a contradiction in terms. However, the proliferation of new liturgical forms in this present century has gone forward at such a surprising pace that questions can and do arise regarding our Anglican identity once so closely associated with shared liturgical formularies inherited from past centuries.

It was for that reason that the Consultation was invited to examine some very fundamental questions regarding our liturgical traditions and their relation to the Church perceived as a priestly people, constituted by the Gospel.

Not all the presentations (let alone the discussions) at the Consultation are represented here. Nonetheless, the papers that could be accommodated to the scope of this publication reflect, it is hoped, the principal themes with which the Consultation wrestled.

In the first of these papers, 'The Formative Character of Liturgy', David Holeton sets forth the situation that confronts us with the recognition that the classical language of the Book of Common Prayer in many ways describes a world other than that in which we live today, while our dependency upon the liturgy for our formation continues undiminished.

The meaning of liturgical formation has been deepened and enriched with studies in early initiatory patterns, and especially a renewed appreciation of the catechetical process and its importance for the Christian's sense of priestly responsibility to the world. Following the Vatican II, these studies led to the Roman Catholic Rite for the Christian Initiation of Adults (RCIA) and the restoration in many places of the catechumenate as an extended process of Christian formation. The second paper, 'The Catechumenate: A Case Study', by Robert Brooks, examines from the perspective of pastoral experience the adoption by the Episcopal Church of the liturgical framework for such a restored catechumenate and its promise for a deepened sense of baptism as sharing in Christ's priesthood.

The early Church's understanding of the *laos* in its totality as the locus of Christ's priesthood, and the gradual clericalization of the Church, is traced in the third paper, 'The Liturgical Ministry of the Laity', by Bryan Spinks. This provides a background for consideration what the liturgical ministry of the laity might mean and how that is being addressed in recent liturgical reforms. His views, those of an ordained presbyter, are balanced and expanded by Daphne Fraser, in 'The Liturgical Ministry of the Laity: A Lay Comment'.

Contemporary understanding of the Church as a priestly people has posed some new questions regarding presbyterate and episcopate and their relation to the liturgical community, especially where there are insufficient clergy; and it is reported that such a question will be before Lambeth Conference this year. It is examined by Paul Gibson, in 'Liturgical Presidency', with special reference to the issues presented in provinces of the Church in the Third World.

Shortage of clergy, however, is not the only liturgical question before the Church in the Third World. Here, especially, the appropriateness of liturgical forms forged from sixteenth century materials in seventeenth century England is raising a vast number of questions that cry out for serious address. Many of those questions receive that serious address from Elisha Mbonigaba. His paper, 'Indigenization of the Liturgy', poses afresh the problem of broad liturgical community in the face of the linguistic and cultural variety of Africa.

This essay, however, only writes large the fundamental problem of cultural diversity addressed by the whole Consultation and by the whole Church today. The seriousness of this 'distancing' of the Church's liturgy from its surrounding culture and from those to whom we are to proclaim the Gospel is addressed as well by Donald Gray, In the concluding paper, *'Ite, missa est,* Liturgy and the Church in Mission', he reflects upon the tendency of Anglican worship to close in upon itself, rather than to send us out, 'to love and serve the Lord'.

The members of the Consultation came from many parts of our planet, and their presentations, while on assigned topics, were prepared without previous discussion. There is not here a polished, balanced address to a single issue. Rather, these essays reveal some specialists' engagement with a complex of problems before the Church today, problems that stem from our concern to make good on the promise of a liturgy that is truly the priestly act of one Body of Christ, from Australia to Scotland, North America to Uganda, and at every time in every place the authentic act by which we, whatever our culture, know ourselves to be bound together as the People of God.

# 1. The Formative Character of Liturgy

## by David R. Holeton

As Anglicans, we have been formed and nurtured by our liturgical texts to a greater degree than perhaps any other communion of the western church. For over four hundred years we have been the people of the Prayer Book and have prayed and re-prayed the liturgical texts in a language we have claimed to represent the vernacular. Yet only rarely have we reflected on the power the liturgy has to mold us into who we are while all the while paying homage to 'our incomparable Prayer Book' and the majestic beauty of its language. The Prayer Book has been the architect that has drawn the parameters within which we have been able to name God, to define our own Christian communities, and to construct a paradigm within which we are able to engage the world. In short, the liturgy is central to our self-identity as Anglicans and is instrumental in directing us in our search for a future as a communion.

To engage that assertion I would first like to examine a maxim which is widely used by those involved in the liturgical renewal that is having such a wide-spread effect on our communion and then to look at a few specific examples of how liturgical renewal has changed the perceptions of individuals and communities. First the maxim. *Lex orandi, lex credendi:* the law of prayer is the law of belief.

While the idea itself was first systematically expounded by Prosper of Aquitaine, its roots are much older and reflect an ongoing dialectic in the life of the Church in which the prayer of the faithful informs the systematic development of the faith of the Church and that faith, in turn, corrects the *lex orandi.* (The contemporary liturgical renewal in the life of the church is a particularly good example of the latter; a process in which medieval, reformation or even more modern liturgical texts are re-examined through the lens of contemporary biblical and patristic theology.) The effect on the life of the churches is, once again, to take their liturgical texts as a primary *locus theologicus.* As such, the Christian community assembled in prayer is engaged in 'doing theology'. What, and how, they pray is a primary theological and liturgical catechesis and provides the structure through which they come to know God, themselves, their community and the world in which they live. As such, the liturgy provides the basic resources to enable Christians to engage life in an integrated manner. The liturgical tools with which they work (both text and sign) have the potential either to open up the imagination and draw the individual and community beyond themselves or to provide such a monochromatic diet of signs and images that the effect is to starve the imagination and to drive individuals and communities inward. Good liturgy does the former. The latter, because of its propensity to fetter the human spirit, barely deserves the name liturgy, but is a phenomenon with which most of us are only too well acquainted.

To illustrate this I will draw on a variety of examples, some from our common tradition (The Book of Common Prayer) and others from the contemporary revision I know best (the Canadian *Book of Alternative Services*). When I cite the latter, I am aware that there are identical—or at least very similar—texts which will come to mind for those who have been engaged in the renewal of liturgical texts in their own provinces.

Before entering into a comparative study of traditional and contemporary texts, I would like to invoke one example from our common past because it contains within itself much of what is germane to the argument as it develops. In the 1662 BCP (following 1549 and 1552) the first bidding in the baptismal rite begins 'Dearly beloved, forasmuch as all men are conceived and born in sin . . .'. The statement is an attempt to assert the reality of original sin. What was 'heard' or misunderstood by the average parents presenting their infants for baptism was not, however, that the ostensibly 'innocent' child being presented was born into a broken and sinful world but, rather, that the very act of begetting the child was in and of itself sinful. There is a long history of parents balking at this assertion and refusing to seek baptism for their children because of it. The place given to human sexuality in Anglo-Saxon culture has been, at least to an extent, formed by this text as popularly misunderstood. It is little wonder that in all the twentieth century revisions of the BCP more effort was devoted to nuancing this line than there was to any other sentence inherited from earlier Prayer Books.[1] It is not only the present generation of liturgical reformers who have been aware of the power of the liturgical text to form attitudes both positively and negatively.

IMAGING GOD

If we turn to questions of our own day, the power of the liturgical text to form us is, perhaps, even more obvious. This is, in part, because there is an increasing gulf between the world view of the traditional Prayer Books and that of our own time. The first Prayer Books, as products of their own age and culture, presumed creation as a given and largely proceeded to ignore it. The political order was perceived as static and those in positions of power were assumed to be there as an act of the manifest will of God. Social mobility was unknown and each

---

[1] A glance at some alternate texts gives us some insight into how various provinces chose to maintain the theological content of the statement while eliminating the offending clause:

England 1928: 'Beloved in Christ Jesus, seeing that all men are from birth prone to sin, but that God willeth all men to be saved, for God is love . . .'.

United States 1928: and India Proposed 1952: 'Dearly beloved, forasmuch as our Saviour Christ saith None can enter . . .'.

South Africa 1954: 'Seeing that all men are born with sinful nature . . .'.

Canada 1962: 'Dearly beloved in Christ, seeing the God willeth all men to be saved from the fault and corruption of the nature which they inherit, as well as from the actual sins which they commit . . .'.

individual was expected to observe the duties of state concomitant with his or her social status. The language in which God is addressed confirms and re-inforces this world view. A quick glance at the inherited Prayer Books or at any Prayer Book concordance reveals God language that is extremely limited and monochromatically hierarchical and patriarchal. When compared to the language used of God in Scripture only a small fraction of the available metaphors are used. In short, when compared with the inherited tradition of both Scripture and the Early Church, the Prayer Book language for God is extremely limited and is selected in such a fashion (either consciously or unconsciously) that it re-inforces a Tudor world-view with all of its limitations.

Demand for a revision of the way in which we address God ought not to come only from those interested in liberation theology or feminism but from all those who wish to be faithful to the tradition as a whole. The effect of addressing God language seriously can be stunning. It is both liberating and transforming. Like gazing at a ray of light as it passes through a crystal, the beholders are breathtaken, not so much because they see something new, but because they see something that has always been there but now see it for the first time. In this category would fall God language that evokes images of covenant, grace, justice, partnership in creation and the feminine amongst others. Psalm Prayers 53 and 82 have some of that effect:

> 'God of the oppressed, we pray for all those who suffer injustice at the hands of indifferent or cruel rulers, especially for the innocent victims of war. Give them strength and patience, and hasten the day when the kingdoms of this world will own the perfect law of love, made known in Jesus Christ our Lord.' (BAS, 772)

> 'Strength of the weak, Defender of the needy, Rescuer of the poor, deliver us from the power of wickedness that we may rejoice in your justice now and forever, through . . .' (BAS, 816).

The language used is certainly not unfamiliar, in that it is drawn directly from Scripture, but it is new to Anglicans in the context of liturgical prayer. God becomes involved in human affairs in a way to which we are unaccustomed and the relationship between liturgy and life is strengthened. When prayers that make this relationship explicit are prayed as a regular part of the life of the Christian, the irrevocable union between prayer and activity in God's world becomes ingrained in the life of Christians.

LITURGY AND SOCIAL JUSTICE

It is in this area of social justice that we encounter some striking examples of the contrast between traditional and contemporary texts. The prayers proper to the Feast of the Holy Innocents are particularly notable. The traditional collect reads:

> 'O Almighty God, who out of the mouths of babes and sucklings hast ordained strength, and madest infants to glorify thee by their deaths: Mortify and kill all vices in us, and so strengthen us by thy grace, that by the innocency of our lives, and constancy of our faith, even unto death, we may glorify thy holy Name; through . . .'

The prayer begins with an assertion that in our age borders on blasphemy ('madest infants to glorify thee by their deaths') and then proceeds to spiritualize the event ('Mortify and kill within us'); invoking a clever word-play ('the innocency of our lives'), we ask that we too may glorify God. Gone is the horrific reality of the slaughter of babies or any appeal to God's righteous justice. It should not be surprising to find that Christians living in a post-holocaust, post-Ethiopian world have difficulty in praying this prayer. We can no longer imagine God being glorified in innocent death nor can we allow such events to pass without yearning for the intervention of a God of justice who we believe calls us to stand in solidarity with the poor and marginalized.

It is not surprising that the old prayer has given way to prayers of this type:

'Almighty God, our heavenly Father,
whose children suffered at the hands of Herod,
receive, we pray, all innocent victims
into the arms of your mercy.
By your great might frustrate all evil designs
and establish your reign of justice, love and peace,
through . . .'

(Holy Innocents, Collect, BAS 398)

'Merciful God,
accept all we offer you this day.
Preserve your people from cruelty
and indifference to violence,
that the weak may always be defended
from the tyranny of the strong.
We ask this . . .'

(Holy Innocents, Prayer Over the Gifts, BAS, 398)

Similar themes emerge in other new texts:

'God of truth, protector of your people, come to the aid of all who are poor and oppressed. By the power of your life-giving word lead us in the ways of peace and integrity, and give us the help we long for in Jesus Christ our Saviour.'

(Psalm Prayer 12, BAS, 717)

'O God, bring our nation and all nations to a sense of justice and equity, that poverty, oppression, and violence may vanish and all may know peace and plenty. We ask . . .'

(Psalm Prayer 72, BAS, 798)

While it might be argued that these prayers are used only occasionally, they serve to underscore a more general awareness of a world being transformed and renewed, which is a theme of many of the new eucharistic prayers. Those who are familiar with the general eschatological vision of the eucharistic prayers, cannot be but affected by the particularity of the other prayers:

'Pour out your Spirit upon the whole earth
and make it your new creation.
Gather your Church together
from the ends of the earth into your kingdom,
where peace and justice are revealed,
that we, with all your people,
of every language, race and nation,
may share the banquet you have promised;'

(Eucharistic Prayer 4, *BAS*, 213)

'In the fullness of time,
reconcile all things in Christ,
and make them new,
and bring us to that city of light
where you dwell with all your sons and daughters;'

(Eucharistic Prayer 3, *BAS*, 200)

The long-term effect of these prayers is not inconsiderable. Just as the Prayer Books formed a paradigm in which the social reality was a positive given, the new texts cast serious doubt upon the ultimate goodness of any given social order (particularly one marked by social injustice or entrenched separation based on gender, race, class or education) and look towards God's fulfilment of all things in the reign of Jesus Christ.

In my own church I have seen parishes' social consciousness transformed through hearing liturgical texts that summon the faithful to participate in their baptismal vocation to be the agents of that kingdom in which the values of this world are overthrown. That transformation has been not only attitudinal but has also found itself being worked out in concrete ways, both social and political. (For example, one older woman I know was led to found a branch of Amnesty International in her parish because of repeatedly hearing a form of the Prayers of the People that remembers victims of torture and political prisoners.)

The power of liturgical texts to form a vision of a new society cannot be underestimated. Again, this is not a new insight; we need only remind ourselves that the English clergy during the Indian Raj were advised not to use the Magnificat at Evensong because of its potential to cause social unrest!

'Source of all life, you have brought us to new being through the waters of baptism. May your love shown in our lives become a wonder and a beacon of hope to the whole human family.'

(Psalm Prayer 114, *BAS*, 863)

POSTURE AND GESTURE
The Latin liturgy inherited by the first drafters of our Prayer Books had fallen into a sorry state. As liturgy it was highly clericalized and reflected the general attitude that ministry was solely the possession of the clergy. All the great acts or

signs that had played such an important role in the liturgical life of the early church had either become so clericalized or vestigial that any sign value they had once had had either vanished or become irreparably obscured. It is not surprising then that the authors of the Second Prayer Book of Edward VI (basically what was to become 1662) abolished the few remaining gestures and produced the most clericalized book to figure in our tradition. The loss of those signs and the radical clericalization of the liturgy has done considerable damage to the way in which we as Anglicans have come to understand our relationship to one another in community as well as the way in which we perceive ministry. The restoration of some of those traditional sign-acts and the renewed seriousness with which we take ourselves as embodied beings are having some profound consequences in these two areas.

By the time the Prayer Book reformers received the Latin rite, kneeling rather than standing had become the normative liturgical posture for the laity. While this was in itself an innovation it sat well with a reformed piety that was heavily penitential and in which the laity were passive spectators kneeling while the minister didactically declaimed the liturgical text. The passion-centred prayer of consecration did nothing to suggest that any of this was inappropriate. In the light of this there is little wonder that, until the past couple of decades, ministry has been equated with the clergy and liturgical ministry was reserved either for the ordained or for a select number of lay people who dressed as if they were ordained. It is not surprising then that many lay people balked at the idea of the ministry of the whole People of God. Liturgical posture and the restrictive character of liturgical ministry put the lie to any renewed theology of ministry. The increasing tendency to encourage the whole community to stand in solidarity with the presider not only makes intelligible the line from the eucharistic prayer, '. . . giving thanks that you have made us worthy to stand in your presence and serve you', but also says strongly that *the celebration of the eucharist is the work of the whole People of God,* and not an activity of the clergy done on behalf of a passive laity. As one of my students commented, 'Kneeling is simply an inappropriate posture for a joyful act of thanksgiving. The body language is just all wrong.'

The restoration of the offertory procession, not in some vestigial form but as visible movement of all, or a large number, of the community towards the holy table bearing not only gifts of bread and wine but other gifts that will be used for the work of the church in the world, underlines the priestly character of all those who have been made new by water and the Spirit.

The recovery of the *orans* position for prayer (hands open and uplifted) has had a similar effect. In the rediscovery of a gesture that was once the common possession of all Christians, but which fell into the hands of the clergy and charismatics, many are finding a palpable sense of openness to God while offering the acceptable sacrifice of praise and thanksgiving.

Perhaps the most dramatic sign to have been recovered is the sign of peace. This gesture, more than any other, has taken Anglicans out of the isolationism that has so often characterized our worship. It has made it quite impossible for any of us to say that we can love God but not love (let alone acknowledge) our neighbour. Where the gesture is taken seriously it has not only become a means of reconciliation between members of our own communities, but it has also helped us learn the difficult lesson of what it means to make peace with those from whom we might choose to remain estranged and, through the imperative of making a gesture of reconciliation, glimpse, if only fleetingly, what it is to be a member of the peaceable kingdom.

It is at the level of gesture and act that we experience most deeply what it is to play at being members of the kingdom. In playing, the liturgy becomes the *antipasto* of the kingdom. Having had the foretaste we cannot wait until we have it in its fullness. Yet in playing, we are slowly transformed into what we play at, being like children who learn what it is to assume particular adult roles simply by playing at them over and over again. What at first seems to be 'mere play' slowly becomes reality.

CONCLUSION

This paper has only begun to touch on the formative character of the liturgy. Over the past few years as I have travelled from parish to parish and diocese to diocese it has often been like witnessing the birth of an entirely new church. The Anglican Church of my boyhood seems very far removed from the church I live in today. The liturgical renewal movement is a primary agent of that new birth. It has changed the way in which we see God, each other, and the world in which we live. But in changing us it has also equipped us for an active part in the mission to which each of us is called.

Over the past century Lambeth Conferences have acknowledged the unifying character of the Book of Common Prayer (1662). In recent years the Primates have expressed the conviction that, as that book passes into desuetude through much of the Anglican Communion, there is a strong liturgical sense that binds Anglicans together. I would strongly concur with both observations. In the past, 1662 held us together because it expressed a world-view that was congruent with that held by the majority of Anglicans. Its view of God, the community and the world functioned in a symbiotic fashion re-inforcing that world-view and affirming that *what was* was right. That world has passed for most of us and so it should not be surprising that so many Anglican Christians have increasing difficulty in using prayer forms that fight so fundamentally with the way in which we experience God, community and world in our own lives.

Yet there remains a profound sense in which Anglicans continue to be liturgical creatures for whom a liturgical text is fundamental to our self-understanding. Just as our theology was once echoed in the Prayer Book text, so too our contemporary theologies echo lines from our new liturgical texts. The law of prayer remains the law of belief. It is that sense, which runs to the core of our being, that keeps us in the Anglican way. And in coming to acknowledge that, we must not forget that liturgy will always remain a 'priority matter' in Anglicanism whether we acknowledge it or not.

# 2. The Catechumenate: A Case History

by Robert J. Brooks

In the Spring of 1977 a young man appeared one Sunday as a visitor at the Eucharist at All Saints' Church in Baytown, Texas, U.S.A. He had never been baptized and had never been concerned that he had not. Garey Atkinson came to church that day not seeking God but in order to accommodate the Christian friends who brought him and wanted to go on to the beach afterwards. What Garey experienced of the Christian community at liturgy that day convinced him that he wanted to return to that church and explore further this faith. His initial inquiry led him through a year of deeper and deeper searching until he came to the waters of baptism at the Great Vigil of Easter the next Spring. Garey walked into All Saints at just the time that the full process of the adult catechumenate had been restored. He became the first person in the Episcopal Church to pass through a fully implemented catechumenate. It was for people like Garey and for Christian communities anywhere that the catechumenate was restored at All Saints. It was out of profound pastoral concern that those coming to baptism be formed for Christian ministry and that Christian community be reformed that All Saints implemented the catechumenal process. As a result, over the years, the catechumenate at All Saints showed that liturgical formation and education were really unified. As the parish came to view itself as primarily a catechumenal community, the Church always coming into being anew, it saw its life centred in the font and flowing from it. No longer was the parish's evangelism, education, worship, prayer, social justice, etc. seen in separate compartments. They were all interrelated and interdependent in the baptismal mystery. The witness of All Saints', Baytown, made a pastoral claim, supported by that of liturgical scholarship, for the restoration of the catechumenate in the American Church.

The 1979 General Convention of the Episcopal Church adopted a form for 'Preparing Adults for Holy Baptism' (the catechumentate). This form is included in the *Book of Occasional Services.* The catechumenal process is identified as the specific form for preparing adults for baptism. The opening comments on the rite state that,

> 'The systematic instruction and formation of its catechumens is a solemn responsibility of the Christian community. Traditionally, the preparation of catechumens is a responsibility of the bishop . . .'

The rite goes on to define the catechumenate as a

> 'period of training and instruction in Christian understandings about God, human relationships, and the meaning of life, which culminates in the reception of the Sacraments of Christian Initiation'.[1]

---

[1] *Book of Occasional Services,* p.112.

The catechumenate, then, is about formation for being a Christian, about formation for the ministry of the baptized. As Yale University liturgics professor Aidan Kavanagh has said,

'What the Church says about who the catechumens are as they enter the font, is to say what the Church is. It is the source of our ecclesiology'.

## THE CATECHUMENATE: PASTORAL TOOL

The restoration of the catechumenate in the Episcopal and Roman Catholic Churches comes as a response to cultural and societal challenges to Western countries in our time. That is why Lutherans, Methodists, and Presbyterians are also moving toward adopting a catechumenate for their churches.

The Rev Herbert O'Driscoll, sometime chaplain to the U.S. House of Bishops, is one of the most eloquent commentators in describing the collapse of cultural consensus in the West in the last twenty years. He notes that at several times in human history Christians have been called by God to live in the abyss between two eras of cultural consensus. Without the clear supports of culture, Christians had to live with ambiguity surrounding them, supported by trust in God and the identity of their baptism. Father O'Driscoll believes that our own generation in the church has been called to live in the ambiguity of the abyss.

This analysis, confirmed by other commentators, places a pastoral claim on the Church to equip its people to minister in these times. The catechumenate came into being in times of cultural transformation and has been restored to the Church as a pastoral response to meet similar challenges. As the Rev. Henry Breul, Rector of St. Thomas' Parish, Washington, D.C., has said, 'The catechumenate is the Church's "survival kit" into the twenty-first century.' The rise of religious fundamentalism in the U.S. reflects a hunger by many to find absolutes to survive bewildering times. The catechumenate is the Episcopal Church's strategy for validly meeting that hunger and for providing comprehensive hope for the future.

## THE PREVIOUS VERSUS THE CATECHUMENAL MODEL OF CHRISTIAN FORMATION

The previous catechetical model emphasized intellectual agreement more than the quality of one's lifestyle. This model has failed to equip many people to confront the instabilities of contemporary existence. While knowing the liturgical colours of the Church Year might be a nice piece of esoteric information, it would probably not be the first thing that would come to mind for someone who needed to make sense of having lost a job at age 55 due to the industry being devastated by more competitive companies in other countries. The previous model of baptismal preparation had an inquirer come to a priest for some brief period of instruction. If one did not vocally disagree, baptism followed. It was not of primary concern for preparation to focus on God's unique call to that person in his/her story or to equip that person to make sense of life in terms of Jesus' story of death and resurrection.

The catechumenal process emphasizes formation leading to transformation, experience as well as information, and lifestyle (living out the values of the Beatitudes and Last Judgment [Matt. 25.31f.]) as well as theological agreement, all in a liturgical context. This approach can better equip the baptized, as I have seen to this day from former parishioners who are using the methodology gained in the catechumenate to deal with the devastation of the economy in Texas.

## THE SHAPE OF THE CATECHUMENATE
The catechumenate has a four-fold shape that is rooted in the shape of human transformation. The catechumenate is conversion therapy that allows the faith God has given as a gift to each inquirer to ripen to fullness. It respects the timetable of God in that person and never makes people commit perjury by making faith statements about themselves which are not true at that time. God leads the catechumens through the stages of pre-catechumenate/evangelization, catechumenate, candidacy culminating in baptism, and mystagogia (sacramental catechesis/incorporation). The community puts itself at the service of the unique call, timetable, and story of each catechumen rather than processing them on some sort of standard assembly line. The four-fold shape provides a framework in which the conversion therapy takes place.

## THE CURRICULUM: OUR STORY—JESUS' STORY
The catechumenate equips people with a language and story to make sense of life. By facilitating the interaction of each catechumen's story with the story of Jesus dead and rising, as unfolded in all its richness week by week in the lectionary, the catechumen comes to see his/her own story as Jesus' Paschal Passage infleshed in him or her. The curriculum is the story of each catechumen interacting with the lectionary. Aidan Kavanagh says that catechumens are 'marinated in the Word'.

This 'marinating' takes place in the catechumenal milieu of prayer, worship, and works of social justice. Catechumens are not only introduced to salvation history in the scriptures, but also are taught Christian prayer, attend worship regularly, and are assigned to ministry with the poor and powerless. The interplay of meeting Jesus in the poor, in scripture, in prayer, and in worship, schools the catechumens and forms them as Christians. It provides their 'survival kit' resources.

Sponsors can testify at admission to candidacy for baptism that their catechumens are people of the Word, of prayer, or worship, of justice. The catechumenate takes us 'back to basics' and shows us that these four marks are essential to the life of each baptized person. Prayer, scripture, social justice, worship are not just for some but for all. Baptism restores a unifying vision to parish life by centring it at the font. As John the Deacon wrote in 500 A.D., 'Baptism tells us who we are and who we are becoming'.

## CONTRAST OF PREVIOUS VERSUS CATECHUMENAL MODEL
The previous model for Christian initiation catechetical formation was programme-orientated, cerebral, based on a nine-month school-year model of

instruction. Its timing was indiscriminate and produced a graduation (elitism) result at the end of the 'hoops'. Its stress was indoctrination only.

The catechumenal model is journey/process-orientated. It is conversion therapy that facilitates a maturing in faith and includes the experiential (prayer, worship, social justice, scripture). Its timing involves communal discernment of readiness. It is initiation as the beginning of a lifestyle with more of the same, not a graduation from the Church. The catechumenate forms people for regeneration regularly—a way to *be* the Church.

## PRESUMPTIONS OF THE CATECHUMENATE

The catechumenate presumes education in the milieu of liturgical formation:
1. This process is a 'flesh and blood' experience of Church. It is not about indoctrinating people with the priest's favourite abstract theology of Church. It is about bringing catechumens up close to the life of the community where they see us, 'warts and all'. It is, therefore, unhesitatingly incarnational.
2. The catechumenate presumes communal participation in the process and in fact. The Church means people, so the ecclesial dimension is respected.
3. The catechumenate affirms that God has already been at work in the inquirers before they come. God will direct the process while they are in the catechumenate, and God will reveal when the time is ripe for candidacy.
4. The catechumenate insists that ritual must speak the truth about the journey and God's gracious generosity. This means that catechumens are not required to make faith statements that are untrue of their point on the journey at a given time. It also means that full symbolism (use of copious amounts of water in baptism) is their pastoral right at the time of initiation.
5. There are catechumenal implications in every other facet of catechesis and sacramental preparation. The catechumenate points to the need to create mystagogical communities in our parishes so that the very rhythm of parish life continually draws out the inexhaustible depth of meaning of our baptism throughout life. Those who have been baptized at whatever age, those who have lapsed since baptism, or those who were baptized in another tradition should find that parish life evokes from them new insights into the meaning of what was already given once-for-all in their baptism. The Standing Liturgical Commission has approved parallel rites to the catechumenate for baptized and unformed adults.
6. The catechumenate is also mutually beneficial to both catechumens and community. They draw faith out of each other.

## INITIATORY NORMS OF THE CATECHUMENATE AND BAPTISM

The restoration of the catechumenate has influenced the understanding of initiation:
1. Initiation has a paschal nature.
2. Initiation is a unitive rite with a tri-fold nature (water rite, pneumatic rite, eucharistic [eschatological banquet] rite).

3. Conversion has an adult nature and is most richly manifested in adult ritual celebration.
4. It is the corporate responsibility of the Church to participate in the process/journey (i.e., laity, bishops, priests, deacons, sponsors, catechists).
5. The bishop is restored to the role of 'Icon of God' (shepherd) in the preparation of catechumens and the celebration of the rites along the way (especially candidacy/initiation).
6. The Lenten Season is restored to its original initiatory character as a pre-baptismal retreat.
7. The catechumenate concretely manifests the new creation and the new humanity.

PARALLEL PROCESS FOR THE BAPTIZED
The 1985 General Convention of the Episcopal Church mandated the Standing Liturgical Commission to develop 'materials and suggested guidelines for the implementation of a practical catechumenate with experimental use in pilot parishes'. In fact, several dioceses have restored the catechumenate with pilot parochial programmes. As a result of these experiences and others the Standing Liturgical Commission has approved a series of rites for 'The preparation of Baptized Persons for Reaffirmaion of the Baptismal Covenant'. These rites parallel the formation process of the catechumenate and echo its principles. Like the catechumenate, the 'presentation of Baptized persons', is composed of catechetical stages that culminate in the celebration of rites. Like the catechumenate, the rite of Preparation uses the Lectionary as its story intersects with that of the candidate for its curriculum. In the case of the baptized the encounter with the Word is mystagogical in character. Like the catechumenate, the rite of Preparation forms the uncatechized in the four-fold *milieu* of scripture, prayer, worship, and social justice. Both rites run parallel in providing an incarnational, ecclesial formation.

Several principles were enunciated with regard to the relation of the two formation processes: (1) Catechumens are to be defined as including only the unbaptized; (2) The baptized who are lapsed from the Church or uncatechized are in no case to be regarded as catechumens or be prayed for with texts developed for catechumens; and (3) the rites for catechumens and the rites for the baptized preparing for reaffirmation should occur on different occasions in the liturgical assembly.

Another pastoral request came to the Commission from several places. It concerned a rite for parents. As a result, the commission approved 'The Preparation of Parents and Godparents for the Baptism of Infants and Young Children'. This rite parallels the shape and principles of the catechumenate as another example of educational formation in the context of liturgical celebration.

CONCLUSION
Because of a deep pastoral concern for equipping the Christian people to live in ambiguous times, the Church has provided a rich initiatory *milieu* continually to form its people. Equipped with its 'survival kit' the Church may better engage in its mission to serve and give hope to the world.

# 3. The Liturgical Ministry of the Laity

## by Bryan Spinks

When asked to speak on the subject of this paper, my initial reaction was to question whether a presbyter who is also a professional liturgist was the best possible exponent. Liturgy is often experienced very differently in the pew from how it is either in the sanctuary or at the scholar's desk. There is the danger, therefore, that my words will bear little resemblance to the real experience of many of the laity.

I want to consider the topic in three sections; first, a brief historical overview of what has been the liturgical ministry of the laity at various times in the past; second, a reflection on some aspects of Anglican liturgy; and finally some remarks or observations on what I have chosen to call 'liturgy through the looking glass'. But, by way of introduction, something needs to be said about the term 'laity'.

The development of the term laity to designate a group distinguished from ordained church officers is usually traced to Clement of Rome, where he makes brief reference to the participants in the liturgy with the assertion:

'the layman *[ho laikos anthropos]* is bound by the lay *[laikos]* ordinances.'[1]
G. H. Williams commented on this:

> 'in assigning the layman a liturgical role along with but subordinate to that of the presbyters and that of the deacons ("Levites"). Clement was at once reflecting general Greek usage of the word "lay" and turning it in a specifically Christian direction.'[2]

But, as Stephen Neill pointed out, the term 'laity' actually covers several different groups.[3] Neill himself distinguished three groups: those who 'live by the Gospel', by which he meant those in minor orders and those living the Religious Life; those who are heavily involved in Church activities, but are not dependent upon the Church for their livelihood; and thirdly, those who quite definitely live in the world, but receive inspiration and instruction from the Church. Neill's divisions are open to question, and it is difficult to understand the wedge he drives between the second and third groups. However, from the point of view of liturgical ministry, those in this first group have had and continue to have a rather fuller role than other members of the laity. Generally in this paper it is not this first group that I have in mind, but those whom Neill classed in the other groups.

## 1. OVERVIEW OF THE PAST

From the point of view of official Judaism, Christianity arose largely as a lay movement. Yet although Jesus was not himself of priestly descent, Christians

---

[1] I. Clement 40.1.
[2] G. H. Williams. 'The Ancient Church AD 30-313', in ed. S. C. Neill and H-R. Weber, *The Layman in Christian History*, (SCM, London, 1963) pp. 28-56, 30. Up until this time Greek Usage was as an adjective to distinguish the mass of people from the leaders. The LXX applied it to things rather than to people. Clement uses it for both people and things.
[3] Neill, *ibid.*, Introduction, pp. 15ff.

hailed him as the true High Priest, and, by incorporation, themselves also as true priests. Vincent Donovan writes;

'In that one supreme moment in his life when Jesus did offer sacrifice once for all, he gathered into himself the whole meaning of priesthood and sacrifice, and obliterated forever the need of a priestly caste. The result of that action and his entirely original contribution was, for the first time in the history of religion, to enable an entire people to be priests. Is this not one of the biggest differences between Christianity and all other religions . . .?'[1]

Although this statement is theologically true, the history of the Church and its liturgy shows that once a distinction hs been made between clergy and laity, the liturgical role enjoyed by the latter was steadily eroded.

In his paper presented to *Societas Liturgica* in Vienna, Paul Bradshaw made the point that in Judaism, within the temple cult, there was little opportunity for the layman.[2] Outside the temple cult, however, there was considerable opportunity. In domestic liturgy the Jewish wife lit the candle and opened the Sabbath with prayer, and the father of the household presided at meal prayers. The Synagogue was essentially a lay movement—and the Ruler of the Synagogue was president and the laity took part in the readings, the chants, prayers, and preaching.

But although Luke-Acts shows that some sections of early Christianity continued to value the temple, the speech of Stephen witnesses to other groups who felt that the temple had no further theological validity; such a conviction we may presume had its origins in the words of Jesus about the temple in Jerusalem and the temple of his body.[3] Worship amongst the early Christian groups was organised either on domestic patterns, or the synagogue pattern, though just how closely these resembled the Jewish parent liturgies is open to dispute. The worship presupposed by Paul seems to have been based on charisms, and he described in a lively manner how all the faithful were active in worship: 'When you come together, each one has a hymn, something to teach, a revelation, a tongue or an interpretation thereof' (1 Cor. 14.16). The problem for Paul was not that there was no active role for any of the people of God in worship, but that worship should be orderly and intelligible. Although no doubt certain people presided, there is little to suggest that in many places there were 'official appointments', but rather, gifts of leadership and organization were recognized by the community. But as Bradshaw points out in the paper already referred to, by the end of the first century, and accelerating in the second, office begins to replace charism, and the ordained ministry began to claim not only presidency of all liturgical rites, but an exclusive right to lead all sections of worship.[4]

The *Apostolic Tradition,* as far as it can be considered a reliable guide to the early third century, still recognizes certain charisms in addition to the ordained

---

[1] V. Donovan, *Christianity Rediscovered,* (SCM, London, 1982) p. 140.

[2] P. Bradshaw, 'Patterns of Ministry' in *Studia Liturgica 15* (1982/83) pp. 49-64, esp. pp. 49-51.

[3] See Nils A. Dahl, 'The Story of Abraham in Luke-Acts', in L. E. Keck and J. L. Martyn, *Studies in Luke-Acts* (SPCK, London, 1968) pp. 139-158; Robert Maddox, *The Purpose of Luke-Acts* (T. and T. Clark, Edinburgh, 1982) *passim.*

[4] Bradshaw, *art. cit.*

offices of bishop, presbyter and deacon: Reader, subdeacon, gifts of healing for example. Thus the laity had certain liturgical functions such as reading or assisting the deacons, and exorcists were to play an important role in the later pre-baptismal ceremonies.[1] But what else was non-clerical?

First, daily prayer. Although the laity were urged to be present at the daily instruction, *Ap. Trad.* allows for prayer at home, as well as in the heart. Thus family domestic prayer, led by a layperson, was observed in the morning and evening; for the more devout (Neill's group 1) other items of prayer were also recommended. But the office here is that of the church, not of clerics and monks.

Second, at baptism, laity were still required to act as referees and sponsors, and also sometimes to instruct. Tertullian maintained that a layman might baptize in the absence of a cleric, but not a laywoman. We can assume, however, that deaconesses and virgins or widows had a role at the baptism of women. The laity, gathered with the bishop, welcomed the newly baptized into the congregation.

At the eucharist the laity brought their offerings, which might include oil, olives and cheese, as well as bread and wine. According to Justin Martyr, the laity stood up and offered prayers (the intercessions) and added *Amen* after the prayers of the president at the eucharist. And of course, to take communion was the goal of their presence, and without them there would have been little need of the president. The eucharistic prayer given in *Ap. Trad.* gives the Sursum Corda, with responses by the laity, and indeed, the prayer is offered on behalf of the whole ecclesia by the bishop. Various chants (e.g., in some places the Sanctus) allowed the laity to take a greater part in the liturgy. Preaching was also at one time a lay possibility, exemplified by Origen, and in Syria in the fourth century by Asterius the Sophist. *Apostolic Constitutions* orders that 'even if a teacher be a laic, still if he be skilled in the word and reverent in habit, let him teach . . .'

Gradually however the theoretical and practical liturgical ministry of the laity was reduced as the clerical orders came to regard the liturgy as their own private privilege and major function. No psalm written by an individual Christian was to be sung in church, and the l;aity were to sit 'quietly and seemly' in their places.[2] The widows, even if learned, were not to baptize nor to teach men.[3] The office of deaconess was to fall into disuse.[4] Laymen in emergency might still baptize; but more and more the liturgical opportunities of the laity were reduced. It is true that they still had psalm-singing, hymns and responses – though even here the cantor or a choir became their surrogate. In theory the laity never lost the right of electing or approving their bishops. However, as bishoprics became tied to property and power, so this role became the privilege of only certain laymen who had a vested interest in such appointments. In the West, where Latin was retained as the liturgical language rather than the barbarous European vernaculars,

---

[1] For this role, see H. A. Kelly, *The Devil at Baptism* (Cornell University Press, Ithaca and London, 1985).

[2] *Apost. Canons,* Canon 40.

[3] Statuta, c. 99 and 100 (Bruns, Canones I).

[4] A. G. Martimort, *Les Diaconesses, Essai Historique,* (C.I.V., Rome, 1982). For the restoration in the Church of England, J. Grierson, *The Deaconess* (Church House, London, 1985).

the only liturgical role available for all but the educated was as passive witnesses to what was now the work of the clergy. W. H. C. Frend rightly wrote:
'Not very much remained of the "royal priesthood" shared by all members of the People of God of the first three centuries . . . The elevation of the priesthood to the status it was to hold throughout the Middle Ages was the natural consequence.'[1]
Is this picture exaggerated? Perhaps. Educated lay people were able to fulfil the role allowed them in the liturgy, and all the laity could still take part through the symbolism, the visual aids, and the drama that the Middle Ages had to develop; it is easy for the twentieth century liturgist to overlook the positive value of this type of liturgy in an uneducated agrarian society. For the educated, the Middle Ages also produced Primers, the heirs of the domestic office. No doubt many exceptions to the picture I have presented could be found; nevertheless, as a general overview, the liturgical role of the laity was reduced to a minimum. There was no attempt to develop the theological and liturgical potential of the priesthood of all believers, other than in groups deemed heretical.

If justification by faith through grace was one of the major rediscoveries of the Reformation, the other was this concept of the priesthood of all believers. The consequence was that in the Reformation Churches, the place of the laity was elevated, in theory, and that of the cleric lowered; in practice only certain laymen enjoyed an elevated position, and many felt that new presbyter was but old priest writ large. Whatever the theological theory of the Reformers, political power and privilege, and a largely uneducated laity severely limited what they could actually attempt. The introduction of the vernacular was perhaps the most important achievement, thus allowing intelligible participation. Luther encouraged the use of hymns and chorales, though again this came to allow a surrogate choir. The Reformed tradition made the mistake of allowing the minister freedom in prayer, with the result that the laity were robbed of any participation other than to listen and utter Amen; this tradition's suspicion with regard to hymns meant that, apart from the metrical psalms, there was little verbal participation by the laity. It will be recalled that at Zurich the Magistrates overruled Zwingli, and the Gloria in Excelsis, Creed and Psalm were not to be recited antiphonically by men and women, but by the deacon alone.

Cranmer's aim is expressed in the preface to the first English Litany:
'And such among the people as have books and can read may read them quietly and softly to themself, and such as cannot read, let them quietly and attentively give audience in time to the said prayer, having their minds erect to Almighty God and devoutly praying in their hearts the same petititions which do enter in at their ears so that with the sound of the heart and with one accord God may be glorified in his Church.'
According to the Preface of the 1549 Prayer Book, the people had hitherto 'heard with their ears only; and their hearts, spirit and mind, have not been edified thereby'; the new services, being in the English tongue, were 'to the end that the congregation may be thereby edified'.

---

[1] W. H. C. Frend, 'The Church of the Roman Empire 313-600', in Neill and Weber, *op. cit*, pp.57-87, 65-66.

Thus understanding and edification were the basic aims of the Prayer Book. As for the illiterate, they remained still very much an audience; for those who could read, the retention of versicles and responses, the collective confessions, allowed some degree of lay participation. Yet much remained the property of the priest. In subsequent years, the parish clerk and priest performed a dialogue and duet, and the laity had only psalms and (rarely) hymns as their liturgical ministry. Only in the absence of a priest (in the New World, for example) did the layman of necessity take up a liturgical ministry, but usually only to surrender it again once an ordained priest had been secured. Thus, apart from the overseas mission field, it is reasonable to conclude that for most Anglicans, until very recently, the liturgical ministry of the laity was confined to listening, confessing, singing, and occasionally responding.

## 2. SOME ASPECTS OF RECENT ANGLICAN LITURGY

Whether inspired by Christian Socialism, or by the continental Liturgical Movement[1], nearly all recent Anglican liturgical revision reflects one of the fundamental concerns of both these movements, namely the church as the body of Christ. This concern, the corporate nature of the church, is found in Beauduin, Herwegen, and the *Mysterientheologie* of Odo Casel, as well as amongst many of those called 'Sacramental Socialists' by Donald Gray, and the early champions of the Parish Communion movement. The centrality of this New Testament image has been criticized recently, and in particular by the Anglican liturgist, J. B. M. Frederick, who has urged a return to a thoroughly worked out Covenant theology.[2] However, one result of the concern for the image or concept of the church as the body of Christ has been a renewed emphasis on the general priesthood of all Christians, particularly in worship. The restoration of a fuller liturgical role to the laity – not always appreciated by all lay people – is reflected in the rubrics of the new Anglican liturgies.

I begin with the one most familiar to me, the Church of England ASB 1980, though this is certainly not to imply that it is by any means the best or happiest of new Anglican liturgies. First, in the offices, a distinction is made between minister, priest and people. Minister may be lay, male or female. Only the absolution is assigned specifically to the priest, though provision is made for adaptation of the text ('you' is replaced by 'us') for use by others than the priest. The officiant, therefore, is no longer automatically a cleric.

More illuminating for the concept of the body of Christ is the eucharistic liturgy. Here the rubrics distinguish between the president, who must be a priest or bishop, and minister. Note 2 before the service observes that the president presides over the whole service (cf the Ruler of the Synagogue) and says the opening greeting, collect, absolution, peace and blessing as well as the eucharistic prayer. The remaining parts of the service he may delegate to others. In many parishes this is precisely what happens. The laity read the lections, and may

<hr>

[1] E. B. Koenker, *The Liturgical Renaissance in the Roman Catholic Church* (Concordia Publishing House, St. Louis, 1966); Donald Gray, *Earth and Altar* (Alcuin Club, Canterbury Press, Norwich, 1098).

[2] J. B. M. Frederick, *The Future of Liturgical Reform* (Churchman Publishing, Worthing, 1987).

preach; they may lead the intercessions, introduce the confession, and share the peace. The offertory procession is quite common, with members of the congregation bringing up bread and wine.[1] In comparison with 1662, there is much more dialogue in the service.

If we turn to the offices and eucharist in the new Canadian and American books, we find similar (and in many respects much better) provision. The office is led by the 'officiant', and the Canadian book notes;

> *'In the form of service for Morning and Evening Prayer, the term officiant is used to denote the person, clerical or lay, who leads the office.*
>
> *It is appropriate that other persons be assigned to read the readings, and to lead other parts of the service not assigned to the officiant'.*

And concerning the eucharist;

> *'The celebration of the eucharist is the work of the whole people of God. However, throughout this rite the term celebrant is used to describe the bishop or priest who presides at the eucharist.'*
>
> *'Lay persons should normally be assigned the readings which precede the Gospel, and may lead the Prayers of the People.'*

Both the Canadian and American books also provide home prayers for groups or families, and the Canadian book gives Grace for meals, and for the anniversary of a baptism. Thus it encourages the recovery of the domestic liturgical role of the laity found in Judaism, which is also the right of the Christian layman.

Thus far so good. But what of the role of the laity at baptism? Here we find a desire to make the baptism of infants a public ceremony that takes place during the normal worship of the congregation. In England, where in an Established Church many baptisms of infants of the unchurched take place, the congregation (the laity) do not necessarily appreciate what becomes a regular disruption of Sunday worship. Perhaps the corporate responsibility of the church is still a far too clerical concern, and as yet unappreciated by many of the laity.

The ASB valiantly attempts to involve the people. At the signing of the cross all join in; there is a response at the beginning of the blessing over the water, and the congregation again joins in the confession of faith of the church, at the giving of a candle, and a welcome. The Canadian and American books do better; the celebrant asks the congregation:

> 'Will you who witness these vows do all in your power to support these persons in their life in Christ?'

Also, everyone renews the baptismal covenant. But is this enough? The Roman Catholic RCIA sees initiation as giving liturgical expression to a gradual ongoing process, combining liturgical celebration with pastoral and catechetical work, and presupposes the involvement of the laity. Already the Episcopal Church in the U.S.A. is developing a catechetical programme on similar lines. Perhaps other Anglican Provinces have something to learn here concerning the interaction of the liturgical ministry of the laity and the general ministry of the laity.

---

[1] Another practice becoming common is for the elements to be administered by laypersons. Provinces differ, some allowing both bread and wine to be so administered, and others restricting permission to the chalice only. This anomaly needs consideration.

What of marriages and funerals? The former is usually a semi-private occasion, and although the people are given responses, their main function is as witnesses. This may well be their legal function, but there should also be a celebratory dimension. By tradition the priest presides over the vows, taking upon himself what was originally a domestic rite presided over by parents. The western preoccupation with vows and valid marriages would seem to militate against a move to give the laity a greater role in this area. But then, what is the role of the laity at funerals? Often these are a clerical monologue *par excellence.*

What we appear to see in the new Anglican liturgies is a partial response to the concern of the Liturgical Movement to exploit the concept of the body of Christ, and restore active lay liturgical roles. The ordained cleric is becoming again more like the Ruler of the Synagogue, presiding over different parts of worship. It may be therefore that the increasing task of the ordained minister will be to teach the laity about worship, to ensure that it is orderly and dignified, and not vulgar and banal. Much more has yet to be done to articulate the many ministries of the body of Christ, but as Robin Green notes:

'Most Christian congregations are a long way from this vision, and it will require at least another decade of consciousness-raising through lay-training programmes and reformed theological education before we see this vision become a reality.'[1]

3. LITURGY THROUGH THE LOOKING-GLASS

When Alice went through the looking-glass she began looking about and noticed that what could be seen from the old room was quite common and uninteresting, but all the rest was as different as possible. Indeed, the other side of the looking-glass was very different. So far I have been trying to look at the liturgical ministry of the laity from the point of view of the activity of the laity *vis-à-vis* rubrics and prayers. But it is important, I think, not to overlook another dimension of worship, which might be called the passive liturgical ministry. Robin Green, in his book *Only Connect,* writes:

'Liturgy is an activity through which a community celebrates its values, passes on its norms and recreates a sense of its own identity through memory and forgiveness. Liturgy can be described, therefore, as an activity tied up with the complexities of human needs and motivations.'[1]

It is on those last words, 'human needs and motivations', that I would like to focus. And this dimension is accessible only through the liturgical looking-glass.

Let me take an example of what I mean. I have already asked the question, what is the role of the laity at funerals? The Funeral liturgy has responses and readings in which the laity can participate and assist with. For note:

'A funeral is not only a therapeutic experience for the grieving family. It is also an opportunity for others within the congregation to prepare for their own future grief situations. The person who has never attended a funeral until he experiences acute grief is at a great disadvantage in not knowing how people are to act, think, and feel at the time of grief. To remind us again,

[1] Robin Green, *Only Connect,* (Darton, Longman and Todd, London, 1987) p. 129.
[2] *Ibid.,* p. 17.

liturgy is education. The funeral liturgy is a vitally necessary part of our preparation for death and bereavement before they occur. Every person's funeral, whether the person was close to us or not, provides an occasion for all of us to think about a life crisis that, without our participation in the funeral, we might not think about at all.'[1]

Thus, the laity's liturgical ministry at a funeral includes coming before God with grief, sadness, loss, faith and defiance. It may include guilt. Thus in a sense a private para-liturgy of emotional response is quite rightly joined with the official liturgy of the Church.

This can be extended to other dimensions and services. I wish to conclude with two very different examples.

A few Sundays ago we attended our Parish Church at Eaton Socon for the Parish Communion at 9.30 a.m. There was plenty of lay participation, and you could have easily illustrated from this service the sort of participation I outlined in section 2 of this paper. But what you could not have observed from the rubrics and texts was my 3-year-old daughter Claire, who stood on her chair with a Ladybird Children's Hymn Book, singing to her heart's content during a hymn. She can't read; she wasn't singing the hymn that we were singing. But she was singing, caught up in the praise and joy of the worship of God in her own little para-liturgy of emotional response.

At the same time there were many strangers in church because there was a baptism at the parish eucharist. Some of the guests were looking around the church, and appeared to have no interest in the liturgy. Perhaps they didn't. But some were perhaps like Stan in Patrick White's *The Tree Man:*

'What does Stan, in his Sunday clothes, think of in Church? The man himself could not have told. He was confused, because his wife was watching, and the words of worship expected too much. His body too, of which he was partly ashamed, made him kneel with an awkwardness that he did not connect with humility. But he was humbler. When he failed to rise to the heights of objective prayer he would examine himself, or the grain of the pew, finding such flaws in each that there was little hope of correction. At times, though, peace did descend, in a champing of horses' bits at a fence outside, in some word that suddenly lit, in birds bringing straws to build nests under the eaves, in words bearing promises, which could perhaps have been the grace of God.'[3]

Here again is a para-liturgy, far outside the actual expectations of the presbyter and the professional liturgist, yet perhaps valid for all that. Green notes:

'Jesus freed people to take their humanity to God. Could there be a better definition of Christian Liturgy? The freedom to take our humanity to God.'[4]

Perhaps in the end that is what is the important liturgical ministry of the whole *laos* of God, clergy and laity alike.

---

[1] W. Williamson, *Worship as Pastoral Care*, (Abingdon, 1979) p.133.

[2] Green (*op. cit.* p.83) notes that in the ASB rite, no opportunity is given for public confession of sin and an act of absolution; it deprives people of dealing with matters that are central to their health.

[3] *Op. cit*, pp. 66ff.

[4] Green, *op. cit*, p. 101.

# 4. The Liturgical Ministry of the Laity: A Lay Comment

## by Daphne Fraser

I share Bryan Spinks' perplexity on how to present 'the real experience of many laity'. One can only agree with him that the lay liturgical role was 'steadily eroded' through the centuries; one need only refer back to the very different and glorious vision of the lay role in the *Letter of Diognetus* to see this:

> 'Christians cannot be distinguished from the rest of the human race by country or language or customs. They do not . . . use a peculiar form of speech; . . . yet although they . . . follow the customs of the country in clothing and food and other matters of daily living, at the same time they give proof of the remarkable . . . constitution of their commonwealth. They busy themselves on earth, but their citizenship is in heaven . . . to put it simply; what the soul is to the body, the Christians are to the world.'

In England today it is not easy to recognize oneself in this vision. Spinks' paper notes the present lack of confidence in lay people who take up a ministry but thankfully relinquish it when a priest appears. We are used to being marginalized, to being negatively defined: *non*-ordained, *non*-'expert'—at best with a 'general' ministry, or a liturgy tht is only a para-liturgy. The symposium on *The Study of Liturgy* (SPCK 1978) has no reference to the laity. If a layperson has developed a liturgical understanding as part of his/her Christian life, it is in spite of, not because of, most recent material.[1]

I note one particular aspect of current liturgical study that appears to sap lay confidence; it can be symbolized by the use of the term 'Response'. On this definition the laity wait for a clergy word or leading, then say 'Amen' or 'and also with you'. This leads to laziness of mind; e.g. in the Church of England ASB text one cannot distinguish the presence and meaning of the *Pax* because the response to it was (and in the ASB still is) identical with that to the *Dominus vobiscum*.[2] This is not a true example of greater lay participation; and it is certainly not dialogue in any real sense. Two scraps of dialogue presented in 1965 and approved in 1967 (the 'cup of blessing' and the dialogue dismissal) were quietly eroded in 1971 into single priestly statements with lay response – thereby depriving us both of some biblical eucharistic teaching, and of imaginative food.

So what is the lay liturgical role? Obviously the various auxiliary roles our church has evolved are necessary and good. As a layperson I value my opportunity to read, to lead intercessions, to sing in choir or congregation, and thus to

---

[1] There are some exceptions to this in the energetic output of Grove Booklets and Liturgical Studies.

[2] Though the *practice* of the Pax has been improved, this criticism of the liturgical text remains.

be a lay auxiliary within the whole liturgy. In these activities there is an element of leadership that counteracts the negative fears or inferiorities which dog the whole concept of non-clerical laity.

Yet we do not want to become mini-priests, to be put in uniform and restricted to the role of reactors. We need more instruction, because we want to be built up, edified. Whether and how far we can be encouraged to take a fuller part in the 'occasional offices' (they *sound* rather marginalized!) or in baptism is an excellent question. In both marriages and funerals the distinction between the professional and the amateur cause difficulty. In marriages, those who make the sacrament by marrying one another may be in a haze of bliss (or, alas, of alcohol). Despite preparation, they may be unable to add much liturgical meaning to 'I will'. Yet the operative words 'I, A, take you, B . . .' are tenaciously deep in our folk religion because they obviously mean something; the meaning is only slightly enhanced by ASB's reference to God's law and solemn vows.[1]

Again in the case of funerals it is hard to call for any but a mechanical response to be made. The minister may be on his fifth cremation service that morning, or be aware of urgent pastoral duties to follow a funeral that took place well outside his parish; but the participants may be reeling with emotional shock from the loss of a spouse or parent, or may be overwhelmed with the guilt evoked by fear of death. I suspect lay expectations at funerals are high, inchoate, and frequently disappointed; hence laity known to be churchfolk, and perhaps the clergy too, become targets for anger immediately afterwards. The demand for various extra liturgies – memorial services, burying ashes, etc. – may be caused not only by the difficulties of distant relatives in attending a family occasion, but may also witness to these anxieties and frustrations. Here indeed we find 'the complexities of human needs and motivations' and perhaps a bigger evangelical role for instructed laity than they tend to think. Our English shyness in speaking about the departed, or listening to the bereaved, is a real hindrance; we have not implemented our increased knowledge of the psychology of grief and mourning. But further I suggest that our funeral liturgy is rather pale. Might there be a place in it for at least optional judgmental material, and penitential prayers? We were rightly keen in ASB to be positive (e.g. the reminder that Christ overcame the sting of death), but I have heard unregenerate yearnings for 'Man that is born of woman hath but a short time . . . in the midst of life we are in death . . . suffer us not for any pains of death to fall from thee'. In short, I endorse the point made about the need for expressions of guilt.

Spinks suggests we may have 'something to learn concerning the interaction of the liturgical with the general ministry of the laity'. I agree in principle, but must express my lack of lay enthusiasm for some attempts to involve us in, e.g., baptisms. We may speak of fearing to do the wrong thing or of disrupting order and dignity, but our reluctance may be due to more than mere English laziness,

---

[1] A useful element in some French marriage services is a strong emphasis on home-making by the newly-wed, i.e. their duty of hospitality; and in England the new ASB form for reading the banns, i.e. 'that these persons may *marry each other*' is coming helpfully into lay consciousness.

shyness, or dislike of crying infants. Too often we know we shall never see parents or child again; in the urban environment of an established church, there can be little reality to 'involvement'. So the 'corporate responsibility of the church' tends to remain regrettably a clerical aspiration. If, however, the baptized infant does become the younger worshipper, he/she may find some liturgies proposed, ie 'family services', lacking in nutriment. They may indeed serve to entertain man rather than glorify God. They also exacerbate the insider/outsider clash, and the growing-together of the congregation can be at the cost of its mission to the world.

The duty of the *laos* is not only to stand 'before God for the world', for if we laity have truly been purified and edified by liturgy, we – and not least our young Christians – must go out and get our hands dirty in pursuit of our ministry. Here is the real force of Spinks' last point, on being freed 'to take our humanity to God'. If we can say or dare anything before God, we may release our aggressions and fears, and also deepen our perceptions of how God became human through love. And here is the heart of our mission.

The most detailed New Testament exposition of ministry starts from the premise, '*Each one of us* has been given his gift, his due portion of Christ's bounty' (Eph. 4.7ff). *Diversity* of gifts is the work-equipment of the laity in his service. Can this diversity gain a fuller liturgical expression? Starting from it, we may all join ministries and, depending on our Head, we may all attain to maturity and live rejoicing in grace. Meeting in this Academy we might learn from Nicholas of Cusa, who says God contains and transcends all distinctions in a 'concordance of opposites' and that we can know him in 'learned ignorance', i.e. by faith and love. This proper articulation of the varieties of gifts will lead us, lay and cleric alike, to 'the mountain that is Christ'.

# 5. The Presidency of the Liturgy

## by Paul Gibson

Presiding at the liturgy is the subject of a number of discussions at the present time. The tradition that bishops and presbyters are the only possible presiders is being tested (at both theoretical and practical levels) in churches that have assumed it as axiomatic for centuries. The hierarchical organization of the liturgical assembly is questioned in some circles. And the style of presiding is open to revision, partly in consequence of other conversations.

The contemporary conversation on lay people presiding at the eucharist appears to have been introduced by a New Zealand delegate to the Anglican Congress in 1963. Canon F. C. Synge, Principal of Christchurch College, suggested that laymen [sic] be authorized to preside at the eucharist, as well as at baptisms, marriages, and burials, while priests concentrate on teaching, preaching and training for action in the world. His proposal, which assumed a shortage of clergy and the need for a weekly eucharist, was based on his conviction that there are only two orders in the church, bishops and laity, and that every eucharist in the church is essentially the bishop's eucharist. Synge was reported to have suggested that when there is a shortage of priests isolated groups are deprived of the eucharist, 'or, rather, the Bishop is deprived of his Eucharist in such places.'[1] He proposed that the bishop delegate his eucharistizing to laymen who have been approved by the people and their presbyter. Such laymen would remain laymen, unless the bishop decided otherwise. The congregation itself could not delegate because the only eucharist is the bishop's eucharist and only the bishop can delegate.

Synge's proposal and others like it have continued to appear in the Anglican Communion and elsewhere in the intervening years. In 1978 the Lambeth Conference asked a group of bishops to consider arguments for lay members of the Church to be licensed to preside at the eucharist in special circumstances. The group reported that they believed there might be circumstnaces in which it would be justifiable for a bishop to authorize a lay person to preside in his name, with the support of the local congregation, because 'where it is not possible to provide a president the bishop is still responsible for making the sacrament of Holy Communion available'.[2] The report was presented and the section agreed that the subject should not be further discussed.

The subject of lay presidency was considered by the Anglican Consultative Council (ACC-6, Nigeria 1984) in the context of Roland Allen's teaching on mission and ministry, a theological framework that places great emphasis on the freedom of the local Christian community and great faith in the power of the Spirit to foster the local community's growth in Christian life and witness. The Council emphasized the need for indigenous expressions of Christian faith, and

---

[1] *This Is What They Said: The Anglican Congress 1963*, p.20.
[2] *Lambeth Conference Report 1978*, (Church Information Office Publishing, London), p.83.

for a ministry of the whole baptized community in which priests are enablers who do not usurp the active role of other members of the body. The Council weighed the pros and cons of non-stipendiary and 'local priest' ministries and came, finally, to the subject of lay presidency at the eucharist.

The Council identified three solutions to the lack of sufficient priests for celebrations of the eucharist among isolated congregations: administration from the reserved sacrament (which it was admitted would probably not be acceptable in some provinces), lay presidency, and the ordination of a local priest. The Council concluded,

'the Council is convinced that the Anglican tradition of priests presiding at the Eucharist should be upheld. Therefore, the Council at this time expresses a clear preference for the ordination of local priests to meet the need. We commend the subject for further discussion at ACC-7 and the Lambeth Conference of 1988.'[1]

The question of lay presidency continues to be raised, chiefly by bishops of the Southern Cone. It was considered, as suggested, by ACC-7 in Singapore. The following entry appears in the report of ACC-7:

'We endorse the previous view of ACC-6 that the Anglican tradition of priests presiding at Eucharist should continue to be upheld at this time and that licensing by the bishops of a lay reader for the purpose of ministering communion in full should not be encouraged.'[2]

The discussion of lay presidency has led to a number of fresh explorations over the years. What, for instance, is the nature of the eucharistic community and why is it necessary to secure the presence of priest in order to have one? Trevor Lloyd, writing in Grove Liturgical Study No. 9, asked, 'How can it be right for a small group of clergy meeting for Bible study to be regarded as a eucharistic community when a small group of lay people meeting for the same purpose cannot be so regarded?'. Lloyd, somewhat more curiously, went on to ask what specifically is the essential presidential act at a eucharist if we no longer believe that the sacramental significance of the bread and wine is effected in a single moment of consecration.[3] Others have explored the history of presidency at the eucharist, and found it more complex than rigid traditions admit. There appear to have been early and subtle shifts from charismatic to institutional leadership, which suggest that even the role of the bishop cannot be identified with the original strata, and there were processes of development in which presbyters moved from being assistants to the bishop to possessing inherently the right to preside in the community (fourth century), and finally to possess the right to preside even apart from the community (twelfth century).[4]

---

[1] *Bonds of Affection, Proceedings of ACC-6*, Badgary, Nigeria, 1984, (ACC, 1984), p.67.

[2] *Many Gifts One Spirit, Report of ACC-7*, Singapore 1987 (ACC, 1987) p.57.

[3] Trevor Lloyd (editor), Colin Buchanan, Douglas Davies, and Robin Nixon, *Lay Presidency at the Eucharist?* (Grove Liturgical Study No. 9, 1977) p.8.

[4] See Paul Bradshaw, *Liturgical Presidency in the Early Church* (Grove Liturgical Study No. 36, 1983) and Hervé-Marie Legrand, 'The Presidency of the Eucharist According to the Ancient Tradition' in *Worship*, 1979.

It is the opinion of this writer that the question of lay presidency at the eucharist is based primarily on pastoral considerations and assumptions relating both to the sacramental needs of the Christian community and to fresh understanding of baptismal ministry. Some of these considerations and assumptions are probably valid and their validity must be tested and defended when established. However, this first level discussion masks at the same time some difficult and unattractive theological and practical concerns, especially in the area of ministry, which must not be allowed to remain unchallenged. Proposals for the authorization of lay presidency have something like a neurotic quality, they are a surface solution to problems that few want to face. Therapy will involve exploration of both the surface and the depths.

The following are some surface elements that appear as arguments in some proposals for lay presidency at the eucharist.

1. The eucharist should be celebrated in every congregation every Sunday, and there are not enough priests to guarantee the Sunday eucharist in many congregations, especially in isolated places. This is a fact of life, not only in missionary areas where there is a shortage of clergy, but also in historic churches in some first world countries where there are more candidates for the ministry than the church can afford to employ. In Canada, for instance, there are many large parishes with multiple congregations of various sizes that will never all be able to employ resident clergy and which are too far apart to allow one priest to go dashing from eucharist to eucharist each Sunday (even if that were an edifying solution). There are parts of the world where the notion of a well-trained, highly-skilled, resident, professional priest living in each congregation has never been, and will never be, a viable possibility.

2. The eucharist is an act of the whole congregation, not of priest in the presence of the congregation. Even if the presence of a priest is a normal requirement, it should not be an absolute requirement.

3. It seems unreasonable to draw the line between clergy and laity at the point of reciting a single prayer on Sunday mornings. Obviously the extensive training that clergy receive has little to do with presiding at the eucharist, which, as one author has observed, could be picked up by most lay people in ten minutes. (Unfortunately, some clergy preside as though they too had picked up the technique in ten minutes.) The training of clergy is obviously about other matters and it is a waste of their valuable time to tie them up with mid-week celebrations for a handful of people. To attach the whole of priesthood to a cultic act is to give that function an almost superstitious status. As Trevor Lloyd put it, 'If one argument against lay presidency is that it would take away from the ordained man the only specific thing that is left to him alone, does that therefore imply that the main purpose of ordination is to provide eucharistic presidents? If so, we could possibly do it more cheaply than we do it at present'.[1]

4. It is the bishop, not the priests, who is primarily responsible for the eucharist. Furthermore, bishops may exercise this responsibility as they wish (presumably within the order permitted by the larger church).

---

[1] Lloyd, *op. cit.*, p.9.

5. The time has come to recognize and enable lay leadership without suggesting that such leaders must experience a call to life-long vocation that finds expression in ordination.

6. In the light of these and other considerations, bishops should delegate their responsibility to lay presidents so that congregations may have the eucharist each Sunday and priests may attend the tasks for which they were trained.

These proposals and assumptions require some preliminary response. First, I affirm the proposition that the eucharist is the basis of Christian Sunday worship and that it is celebrated by the whole congregation. I know only too well that the goal of a professional priest in every congregation cannot be realized and I would go further and suggest that my attempt to realize it may be injurious to both the church community and the individual who serves within it. However, the true problems begin to emerge when an attempt is made to discuss the nature of the ordained ministry and its relationship with the local community. They become clearer when we realize that many lay people who are prepared to devote much time and energy to leadership in the church would not dream of accepting ordination as it is now understood. And they become serious when all the powers of the church are seen to be invested in a distant bishop who is expected to solve them by passing over the difficulties of the present structure. I believe that lay presidency is only a smoke-screen for deeper questions, solutions for which lie beyond the deadlocks we are reluctant to face. These include:

1. It has become almost impossible in some sections of the church to distinguish between a theology of Christian leadership and the forms in which the ministry has been shaped by history and by the social function that it plays in both church and society. Robin Nixon suggests that ordination to local ministry may be right in principle but complains that it has 'raised many difficulties because of the association in the mind of the man in the pew as well as the man in the street with "being a clergyman". This creates some role confusion for those so ordained and may be something that inhibits a genuinely lay witness'.[1] This is the real rub: priesthood has become a culture within the church, almost a lodge, separated from the *laos* not only by training and skills but also by assumptions and attitudes (both real and imagined) and by the cumulatively significant apparatus of rank, titles, and dress. Clergy (not all individuals, but as a group) are in fact divided from the church and the proposal of lay presidency would spread the wallpaper over that division. On the one hand it would enhance the growing ministry of lay people; it would be possible for a lay person to assume the ultimate symbol of leadership, visible presidency in the Christian assembly, without becoming 'a clergyman'. On the other hand, it would leave the special status and privilege of ordained clergy unchallenged.

2. There is an assumption in much of the literature on lay presidency that priesthood is a matter of professional expertise. Actually, priesthood (eldership) is a matter of pastoral care which may involve expertise of many styles and degrees. Many lay people exercise pastoral care towards their

---

[1] Robin Nixon in Lloyd, *op. cit.*, p.31.

fellow-parishioners and neighbours. The creation of too strong an image of professional expertise among clergy may have contributed to their isolation from the rest of the church community.
3. We have accepted with too little complaint a dislocation of the church's practice of ministry from its liturgical celebration. Hervé-Marie Legrand concludes simply, 'The rule is constant that it pertains to those who preside over the upbuilding of the Church to preside over the sacrament of her unity, over the sacrament which causes her to exist more profoundly in act'.[1] The leader (elders, presbyters, priests) of the local church *are* the ministers, chosen by the congregation, 'with the indispensable assistance of the heads of neighbouring churches'.[2] The shape of the church from Monday to Saturday should be reflected in the shape of its assembly on Sunday. This explains why Schillebeeckx said the early church would have dismissed as perverse the question, 'Could a layman preside?'. 'The decisive element', he says, 'is the acceptance of a president by the church'.[3]

These principles throw into question not only proposals to authorize lay people to preside at the eucharist but also the ways in which priests are deployed for the same function. Parachuting clergy into parishes where there is no resident priest with nothing to commend them but the technicality of their orders, is as perverse as (or more than) the convoluted thinking that would like to arrange for a congregational leader to preside at the congregation's assembly without recognizing the fact that he or she has assumed a presbyteral role. Robert Hovda has argued convincingly that no one should preside in a congregation of which they are not part.[4]
4. Finally, the proposal to authorize lay people to preside at the eucharist abandons the biblical principle that ministry is defined primarily by an act of worship. Anointing, touching, breathing, praying, these are the usual ways in which leadership is focussed and expressed. There is a tendency among the proponents of lay presidency to take refuge in a very high doctrine of episcopacy (and a very high doctrine of canon law) in which the bishop's juridical acts (e.g., licensing) are made equal to the bishop's liturgical acts (e.g., ordination). There is a true way to authorize leaders who have been identified by the local congregation to preside at the eucharist, and that way involves laying on of hands with prayer.

It will be argued that leaders in local congregations may be unwilling to accept such ordination for a number of reasons: they may not want to accept the implications of 'indelibility', they may not feel a vocation to life-long ministry, they may not want to be considered 'clergymen', and they may not feel they have time and energy to be the only presbyter in a congregation.

All these are problems to be overcome, not obstacles to cause despair. The concept of indelibility is historically and theologically suspect and is nowadays

---

[1] Legrand, *op. cit.*, p.436.
[2] *Ibid.*, p.437.
[3] E. Schillebeeckx, *Ministry: Leadership in the Community of Jesus Christ* (Crossroad, New York, 1981) p.51.
[4] Robert Hovda, *Strong, Loving and Wise* (The Liturgical Conference, 1987).

ignored when there is need to reduce a priest to lay status. Legrand, arguing that pastoral care precedes eucharistic presidency, notes that until the thirteenth century, 'deposition returned a priest to the rank of layman in the full sense of term, that is to say, to the situation that was his before his ordination'.[1]

The subjectivity that we attach to the word 'vocation' must be challenged. Legrand points out that among early Christians no one sought the priesthood and some were constrained to accept ordination. 'A vocation', he says, 'is, objectively, the appeal which the community addresses to one or several of its members which it considers suited to the ministry, even if they never wanted it'.[1] Christian communities may still make that appeal, and to more than one leader in their group if that is desirable.

The resistance of some people to be identified with a clerical culture is understandable and commendable. Others may have to be warned against it. The church will never, however, be able to address the isolation of clergy and the rest of the *laos* from each other (reflected in the persistent assumption that clergy are not lay people) until recognition of leadership is extended to actual local leaders in the congregations and is no longer restricted to those who have completed a course of study of several years duration and have passed an exacting battery of professional and vocational tests. The whole of Christian life, from baptism onwards, is a process of formation for ministry, and presbyters—whether paid or unpaid, full-time or part-time—must find their life-style within that whole. A growing body of local leaders who exercise a presbyteral ministry may be of great help to professionals in their pilgrimage.

This, then, is an appeal for serious consideration of the ordination of local leaders in Anglican congregations to both the presbyterate and the diaconate in accordance with their gifts, not merely as an emergency measure to provide the sacraments where they cannot now be offered, but to recover a liturgical celebration of leadership as it rises from within the local congregation and finds the affirmation of the wider church. There will still be plenty of room for clergy with specialized training. (There will also be room for a reconsideration of the structure of the episcopate, because a church with more local leaders may need bishops with smaller dioceses who can maintain a more intimate contact with local congregations.)

There is one situation in which lay presidency at the eucharist is not only permitted but, in the opinion of Tertullian, is mandatory, and that is when a congregation is completely out of touch with (has no access to) ordained leadership. It should, however, be noted that this situation does not call for the substitution of licensing or legal authorization for a liturgical form of authorization. This situation depends on the lack of any possibility of authorization at all. In such cases, according to Tertullian, the local community has the duty to identify its own leaders. Such a leader would be no longer lay, as we understand the term. As Schillebeeckx puts it,

'Anyone who in such circumstances was required by the community to preside over the community (and thus at the eucharist) *ipso facto* became a

[1] Legrand, *op. cit.*, p.431f.
[2] Legrand, *ibid.*, p.437f.

minister by the acceptance of the church: he was instituted, i.e., became the authorized leader of the community.'[1]

Another speaker at the Anglican Congress to which Canon Synge made his proposal was Bishop John C. Vockler of Polynesia. Bishop Vockler spoke of the incredible challenge offered by his situation and the impossibility of meeting that challenge from within a traditional model of episcopacy. He spoke of a longing for creative thought that would provide freedom from the shackles of he presuppositions that had been inherited from the parent churches.

'For many of us still in several parts of the Anglican Communion the division of our dioceses depends on provincial decisions which cannot be made with full awareness and knowledge of our situation, and which inevitably result in the perpetuation of a pattern of episcopacy which should be challenged "at home" but which is certainly disastrous in the churches of Asia, Africa and the Pacific.

'There is a very real danger that we can insist on a mode of episcopal life which costs more than an indigenous church could support, that the prestige of a bishop can be such as to identify him with an alien way of life, and that the normal regulations of episcopal government will be too complicated for our people to follow.'[1]

Canon Synge and Bishop Vockler offered radically different approaches to a problem in ministry that has only continued to grow since 1963. Canon Synge's solution appeared to be more radical and daring, but in fact it was calculated to leave the structure of the ministry unchallenged. Bishop Vockler begged for freedom to release the ministry, in his case the episcopate, from the forms in which it had been shaped by history and the patterns of western society. The recovery of a liturgical relationship between the actual leadership roles exercised in a cngregation and the Sunday assembly would challenge the assumptions that have surrounded the practice of ministry and would solve the problems identified by Canon Synge without substituting legal for sacramental actions.

*　　*　　*

I noted at the beginning of this paper at least two other dimensions of presiding at liturgy that are attracting attention at the present time. Both require some, if shorter, comment.

A major theme of the feminist influence on theological discourse is the need to question a hierarchical model of piety, organization, and liturgical practice, whose roots may be found in the patriarchal assumptions of Jewish-Christian origins and imagery. A society by males, runs the critique, is vertically structured and that vertical structure is codified in imagery and roles that are communicated in styles of worship at the levels of both content and organization. At the level of content, prayers couched in the language of hierarchy suggest that divine infinity is secured by the power and majesty of God in relation to human poverty and weakness. An extreme example, perhaps, is the Prayer for the Queen's Majesty, which combines images of paternity, height and power: 'O Lord our heavenly Father, high and mighty, King of kings, Lord of lords, the only

---

[1] Schillebeeckx, op. cit., p.51f.

Ruler of princes, who dost from thy dwelling behold all the dwellers upon earth
...' There is growing sensitivity to the criticism of hierarchical imagery at the
level of content, which many new liturgical texts reflect.

At the level of the organization of the worshipping community, some critics
contend that the notion of presidency *over* the assembly is intrinsically hierarchical and models residual paternalism, whether the presiding celebrant is a man or
a woman. Some liturgists suggest that shared leadership (not concelebration,
which simply associates co-presidents with the person who presides *over* the
assembly) is more appropriate. When leadership is shared the direction of the
liturgy is in a number of hands, but it is not possible to distinguish one of them as
*primus* or even as *primus inter pares*. The closing liturgy (not a eucharist) of the
North American Academy of Liturgy in 1985 was designed on this model.

It is my understanding from personal conversations that shared leadership
tends to characterize the eucharistic celebrations that have frequently been
celebrated by groups of Roman Catholic religious women in recent years. Sharing may take the form of the community designating a different leader on each
occasion, or it may mean that several or all of those present assume leadership at
different points in the liturgy. In any case, the women involved in these celebrations are laying claim in a very concrete way to the right of a community to its
own sacramental life and that it is the ecclesial community itself that is priestly.
When Tertullian said, 'where no college of ministers has been appointed, you,
the laity, must celebrate the eucharist and baptize'.[1] he probably had an
emergency situation in mind, for instance a church's loss of its ordained leaders
to martyrdom. It would appear, by implication, that some devout Christians in
catholic and sacramental traditions now regard the inability of their church to
change the historically and socially conditioned forms of ministry as constitut-
ing an emergency which demands a similar response.

These movements in thought and practice must eventually have some effect
on the style of liturgical presidency even where liturgy remains relatively
traditional. Liturgical revisions assume that a number of people will be
associated with the presider at a celebration of the eucharist—readers, inter-
cessors, ministers of communion and others. But the very style of presiding itself
is open to change, for the word 'preside' carries connotations of presiding *over*,
and this superiority of the leader is now challenged, on biblical as well as
humanistic grounds. Liturgical leadership must learn the role of the servant, not
in obsequious deference to the rest of the community but in providing strength
and direction from below and from within. Roberts Hovda has written exten-
sively on the subject of liturgical presidency. We may note his words:

> 'Like the rest of the church, the pastor has to be struck to the roots of his/her
> soul by the unimaginable liberty of prayer, the grace of fogiveness, the
> awesomeness of faith. On a more mundane level and practically speaking,
> it is not the pastor who "lets" the congregation in. It is the entire
> congregation, the church, the faith community which "lets" one of their
> number, ordained for this purpose, preside.'[2]

[1] Schillebeeckx, *op. cit.,* p.74f.
[2] Hovda, *op. cit.,* p.74f.

# 6. Indigenization of the Liturgy

## by Elisha Mbonigaba

The purpose of this paper will be to review much that has already been written on the subject of indigenization and then to suggest some areas that may need indigenization.

HISTORICAL BACKGROUND
The Anglican Church in Uganda, and in other parts of Africa, is the result of Church Missionary Society (CMS) activity, which imported all forms of western Christianity and culture. As Fred Welbourn has observed, the Anglicanism of the Church of England was a product of the historical, political, economic, and geographical England of the sixteenth century, and was for home consumption but unsuitable for export. The countries to which Anglicanism was exported presented quite different political, cultural, social and religious contexts.

The assumptions of CMS missionaries and their methodology in trying to convert people were characteristic of all foreign missionaries of mainline churches across Africa. They tried to reach the intellectual and ethical levels of African consciousness without ever appealing to the deeper emotional sphere that could only be expressed through symbols, myths, rituals and exuberant music. They tried to make converts speak and behave like the white man.

Muzorewa quotes a Roman Catholic missionary in West Africa as saying, 'unless the African pagans adopted much western culture and civilization, it was difficult to measure the success of the missionary task' and 'to the early missionaries in the church, the [adoption of western] life style by the heathen was regarded as one of the fruits of conversion to Christianity'.[1]

The first name of the church planted in Uganda by the CMS was the 'Native Anglican Church', but this was changed to 'Church of Uganda' because the term 'Anglican' carried overtones of paternalism. Nonetheless, Anglicanism in the western English sense was adopted as part and parcel of the Christian faith, and up to this moment we are still clinging to those archaic traditions that the Church of England rejected a long time ago. As many writers have observed, Christians—including church leaders (bishops and clergy)—in other parts of the third world have accepted Christian faith along with the 'western cultural drab'.

Schnijder says that bishops in Indonesia are afraid of innovations because they are insecure about the way the world culture is growing and insecure in themselves. This seems true everywhere. There is a fear of losing one's identity.

---

[1] Muzorewa, *The Origins and Development of African Theology* (1985) p.29.

David Holeton also observes that, in spite of encouragement from the Anglican Primates' meeting of 1983 to the third world Provinces to engage in liturgical revision, 'the first generation of indigenous leadership tends to cling closely to the inherited liturgical tradition and only with reluctance strays from BCP 1662'.[1] Holeton does not blame them, but blames 'the missionaries who spread the BCP as the guardian of the essence of Anglicanism and Lambeth Conference which in 1958 pointed to the 1662 BCP as a principal agent for preserving unity'.

AFRICAN LITURGY
The first attempt at an African indigenous liturgy was made about twenty-four years ago. Representatives from all the Provinces in Africa met in Kampala, Uganda, in 1963 and drafted the first African Liturgy. This was commended by a liturgical consultation of Anglican Churches that met in Toronto, Canada, in 1963, to be used on an experimental basis in the then five Provinces of Africa. This was supposed to unify the provinces.

Not many dioceses or provinces ever used the service because it was produced in English and there are few local translations. Another problem was that the African Liturgy was done by a westerner following the Church of South India format. There was nothing African about it. Leslie Brown, the author, could not see 'how the element of spontaneity,' which is an important characteristic of indigenous worship, 'can be given a place in corporate worship, in liturgy'. [2] He wrote, 'the only indigenous form of worship I know in Africa is the fellowship meeting of the Revival groups'.[3] This revival movement in Uganda and East Africa shares the characteristics of African independent movements.

ANGLICAN RENEWALS
Colin Buchanan has published three books about liturgical renewal in all provinces of the Anglican Communion: 1958-1968, 1968-1975, 1976-1984. In his survey he informs us that some Anglican Provinces, especially the English-speaking Provinces, have tried to renew and revise their liturgies. However, none of the third world Anglican provinces has come up with indigenous liturgies. For example, the experimental liturgies of African provinces, e.g. West Africa, Nigeria, South Africa, Kenya, Tanzania, are either modelled after the 1662 BCP or modern English series 2 and 3, or the American BCP 1928, while others, including Uganda, are still using a translation into local languages of 1662. I was interested in his comment of 1975 about the province of the Church of Uganda, my own province: 'The Province of Uganda, Rwanda, Burundi and Boga-Zaire has seen internal disturbance more recently than Nigeria, and there also any slight stirrings towards liturgical reform have been stifled. The Province is in any

---

[1] David R. Holeton, 'Liturgical Revision in the Anglican Communion'.
[2] L. W. Brown, *Relevant Liturgy* (Oxford, 1965) p.13. [The sentence ends, however, 'but I am sure we have to think about this'. Ed.].
[3] *Ibid.*, p.34.

case very attached to the 1662 tradition . . .. It seems safe to forecast that in the year 2000, 1662 will be found most solidly and notably in use in the Province'.[1]

Buchanan observed very few signs of genuinely national cultural patterns in third world revised liturgies. For example, he states that the rubric in the New Guinea Liturgy 1970 mentions the use of bell, drum and rattle twice in the Eucharistic Prayer. He also notes the rubric for the 'Kiss of Peace' in the Korean Liturgy of 1973: 'Each person bows to those standing near him'. These are the only indigenous variants he mentions.

The third world provinces, especially those in Africa, need to go beyond those two rubrics. Africa has a rich cultural and religious heritage. They have rich myths, rituals and symbols, all imbued with religious meaning. The western world is now rediscovering the importance of myths, rituals and symbols to communicate the gospel. They are using them for hermeneutic purposes. Africans do not need to rediscover them. They are part of their culture.

African traditional culture is not pagan or primitive or superstitious as early students of anthropology, missionaries and colonialists used to call it. In fact, it is now being argued convincingly, by both western and African scholars, that if the Christian church in Africa is to survive and be relevant and effective in her mission to contemporary Africa, she has to adapt to the cultural context.

Anscar J. Chupungco has shown us how Christian liturgy has adapted itself to Jewish culture, Graeco-Roman culture, European culture, and he tries to show how Christian liturgy has tried to adapt to third world cultures. He says, 'Adaptation [Indigenization] is not an option, but a theological imperative arising from incarnational exigency. The Church must incarnate herself in every race as Christ incarnated himself in the Jewish race'.[2]

It is by the incarnational principle that indigenization of liturgy has to be done. People should be allowed to worship in their own way. The way they can understand. Having said that, some people would object on the ground that there would be a danger of syncretism or 'antiquarianism' or reviving old pagan things. Indigenization does not necessarily mean 'digging up the religious past', but it has to take into consideration the cultural values and the present realities of social, economic, political and religious factors that influence and condition our life.

AREAS OF INDIGENIZATION

The purpose of this paper is not to give a detailed analysis of African indigenous liturgies such as the eucharistic liturgy that has received much attention in Anglican liturgical renewal. Rather, I will make general observations and cite a few areas where indigenization of liturgy might be addressed.

As we have already mentioned, Bishop Buchanan did not see any genuinely national cultural patterns in the liturgical renewals of the third world provinces. This is a big challenge to the third world. We need to study seriously our own

[1] Colin O. Buchanan, ed., *Further Anglican Liturgies 1968-1975* (Grove Books, Bramcote, 1975) p.247.
[2] Anscar Chupungco, *Cultural Adaptation of the Liturgy* (Paulist Press, New York, 1982) p.5.

cultural heritage and other related disciplines and come up with rites and liturgies that reflect our own unique context without falling into the danger of adopting the now revised liturgies currently being used by English-speaking Provinces, like the English Alternative Service Book (ASB) of 1980 and the Canadian *Book of Alternative Services*, 1985.

Care should be taken not to generalize when trying to indigenize liturgy. Africa and even each state is a multicultural and multi-lingual country. While some of the cultural values, myths, rituals and symbols may be the same, most of them are different and unique to a particular place. To try to make an 'All-African Eucharist', as Roman Catholics have done, by just borrowing different images, prayers, etc. from different peoples of Africa will not make it authentic. Here thanksgiving, epiclesis, anamnesis, narrative of institution, acclamations, intercessions and final doxology are linked with certain rituals of traditional African worship: the offerings of the first-fruits, sacrifices for sin, presentation of the victim for sacrifice. The starting point for each section of the prayer is an authentic prayer from African traditional worship. The images used are from the Duika of Sudan. The African values portrayed are life, fecundity, the ancestors, medicine, and kinship. Certain Christian traditional concepts are 'translated' into African values; e.g. the Holy Spirit becomes 'spirit-medicine of life' and covenant becomes 'pact of blood brotherhood'. The All-African Eucharistic prayer is styled in short phrases, typical of African ritual formulae, and special emphasis is laid on the efficacy of the spoken word.

However, the idea of picking up different images and prayers from across Africa and juxtaposing them into one prayer is like making a jigsaw puzzle, and this is not helpful because not all people in Africa do use the same symbols or prayers in the same way or under the same conditions.

For example, for some cultures a formal pronouncement of blessing is often accompanied by gentle spitting. For such people the spittle symbolizes prosperity and health of humans, cattle and fields. It symbolizes plentifulness of children, cattle, and food. This symbolism cannot be generalized and universalized. In other cultures it may imply a curse or spite.

What I am saying is that cultural symbols or prayers should be used in their own particularity. Language is one of the characteristics that gives a particular people its authentic history and tradition, and it is in the language of the people that liturgy should be expressed; but the problem we have to contend with is the multiplicity of languages in our nations, which have no one indigenous language as *lingua franca* uniting people, other than the foreign languages of English and French.

For example, it would be unrealistic within the economic means available to expect that all the 28 languages in Uganda, or 120 Nigerian and Tanzanian languages can equally have indigenous liturgies developed. There is a need to evolve one indigenous language in one nation that can unite people, being used in commerce, communication and worship. In the case of Uganda, Swahili, which is now used in Kenya and Tanzania, would be the alternative language that could unify Ugandans and link them with their neighbours. In Northern Nigeria ten states have been united by the Hausa language.

Until one language has evolved in one Anglican province, then each diocese has to use its own language and culture. The problem of diversity or the issue of unity, if it means one province or one Anglican Communion doing and using the same liturgy, should not even be our concern. Two writers in the U.S.A. have said, 'The scandal of our present liturgical situation is not its diversity of style.... Diversity is not the problem. The problem is the separation of liturgy from the life of the Christian person and from the life of the Christian community'.[1] I do agree with them. Our concern should be to be faithful to our mission, to make Christianity relevant to the people. So let us look at a few areas that need indigenization.

### PRAYERS

African traditional religious life was characterized by spontaneous, extempore prayers, poured out from the heart to God, expressing the worshippers' feelings, aspirations, anxieties, worries, pain, suffering and joy. Prayers would be in the form of invocations, supplications, blessings, curses, salutations, greetings, and farewells. And, as Mbiti says, these would be uttered 'at any time and in every place'.

The indigenous liturgy would be more relevant if it used this richness of African prayers rather than adapting old medieval or reformation prayers or even the present western prayers in modern liturgies, which are culturally, historically and politically conditioned by the religious piety of their time.

Indigenous prayers would include prayers that would commemorate ancestors or the living dead, because in African society the dead are part of the family. This does not mean that Africans worship ancestors as some western people tend to think, but they are given their special place in the religious life of the society, They affirm the continuity of the society. In the same way, Israel did not worship Abraham, Isaac and Jacob but remembered them as founders of their nation. We Christians remember them not as our national ancestors, but as spiritual ancestors. 'I am because we are; we are therefore I am', is an important African philosophical maxim, which includes the unborn, the living and the dead.

### SPONTANEITY

Worship according to the BCP 1662 is of an intellectual and meditational nature. It seems it was designed for people to remain private and passive without any interaction and involvement with each other. No excitement at all. The atmosphere is dull and quiet. People sit, stand, kneel, close their eyes in a stiff, unnatural manner, fearing to touch the next person. There is a joke in my area which says that Anglicans close their eyes to allow God to pass!

### AFRICAN MUSIC

That kind of atmosphere in worship is unnatural to Africans. Africans love to sing, dance, clap and shout with joy, swaying their bodies or stamping their feet on the floor. Musical indigenization calls for church music and musical instruments that appeal to the emotions of people. Like the Psalmist, using harps, drums, rattles, etc., they would dance and sing with joy before the Lord. Mbiti writes that singing helps to pass on religious knowledge from one group to another and helps to

---

[1] Charles P. Price and Louis Weil, *Living for Liturgy* (New York, 1979) pp.30-31.

create and strengthen corporate feeling and solidarity. The purpose of worship is to bring people together and build them into creative communities. Given that the biggest percentage of the rural community still uses oral communication, singing traditional hymns with traditional music would be an appropriate way of teaching, transmitting and preserving Christian faith. This is the area where the principle of *lex orandi, lex credendi* comes into play. Here, the prayer of people through singing should reflect their faith.

English hymns have their own characteristics, which cannot be translated or adapted to African tunes and rhythms. Western hymns, Christmas and Easter carols that talk of four seasons of the year, snow or winter, or that give western cultural settings, are irrelevant to the African situation.

There are, however, some signs of local composition for church music. In Uganda, a Luganda song about the Ugandan martyrs was composed for the centennial celebration of the Church of Uganda. *Bewayo,* meaning they 'sacrifice' for the Lord, has been included in the Luganda Prayer Book. The problem, though, is that this song cannot be easily translated into the other twenty-seven languages of Uganda without losing its beauty and meaning. This suggests that each culture has to compose its own music.

BAPTISM—INITIATION

Across Africa there are many references to various rituals and ceremonies in connection with pregnancy, childbirth, naming, weaning, and initiation, all of which intend to incorporate and integrate the child and the young adult into a family, a society, and the entire nation.

Symbols and rites performed signify the concept of death and resurrection to full life, they symbolize separation and incorporation. Different marks, some of which are indelible, symbolize identification, incorporation, and membership with full religious and social rights in the community. They link the living and the dead. This African tradition of being incorporated into the community can provide rich liturgical material for Christian baptism.

The ages at which various rites of incorporation are done vary from cultures to culture, but various stages mark the religious journey that begins before actual birth and continues through one's lifetime. In this context, holy communion, the religious symbols shared by those who have been incorporated into the Christian community, the church, could well be shared by children, who religiously would have been incorporated into the community at the earliest age. Confirmation, administered after the age of twelve, would not be a condition of sharing in the Eucharist.

Children understand the mysteries of God and nature, and they are also teachable. When children are denied things, they do not become part of that experience. So children have to be taught at the earliest age what receiving the bread and wine mean, and the religious impression and experience from this teaching and participation will mark them indelibly as they grow.

New liturgies have used the title 'Initiation' for the rite of Christian baptism, which is the rite of naming and incorporation into the Christian church. Initiation in most African societies refers to circumcision and other rites that come at the age of adulthood. This comes after other rites of incorporation that are done at and after birth, like naming and weaning. I am not quite sure whether they would be called initiation, and yet they are very important. An indigenous liturgy of baptism would therefore need to use all symbols of incorporation before and after birth, including naming.

## USE OF AFRICAN NAMES

In African society names are given according to the circumstances in which the child is born, sometimes as an answer to prayer or symbolizing an attribute of God, his love, his care, power, or kindness. Most of them incorporate God's name as an expression of worship and faith in God. Using English names like Smith, Wilberforce, Fred, etc., or even Hebrew names from the Bible, such as Deborah, names which are conditioned by western or Hebrew cultures and sometimes of pagan origin, is irrelevant in a totally different cultural circumstance. Anglicized names were once taken for social respectability. Later, they became political.

Sometimes the English names are a translation of the same family names. A girl could be called Peace Busingye (Busingye means peace) or Grace Mbabazi (Mbabazi means grace), or Hope Bwiringiro (Bwiringiro is hope). There are many examples of such duplication.

Some educated Africans have discarded such English names, given at their infant baptism, in favour of their African traditional names, and a few church people (both lay and clergy) are beginning to use African names, but this is with strong disapproval from the bishops and conservative groups who would not want to lose their western identity. Yet it would be more relevant, pastorally, theologically, and liturgically, to use African names in Christian baptism.

The rite of baptism could use cultural symbols that signify separation from the mother or from the world and incorporation into the community.

## SACRIFICE—EUCHARISTIC SERVICE

The word 'sacrifice' in connection with eucharistic liturgy might put off some people, but any indigenous eucharistic liturgy will have to take into consideration the sacrificial system, which is important in the religious life of traditional Africa. The symbolism of blood in sacrificial systems and in blood relationship rituals is very important. As in the Jewish concept, blood is life.

Sacrificial meals are traditional in which all members participate, binding them with the unborn, the living, and the dead. In this kind of ceremony, worshippers would gather to tell their story for its continual survival.

In the same way, in the Christian eucharist people gather as the family of God and they tell the story of Jesus Christ, the story of the creative and redemptive work of God in Christ, and they tell the story of the church.

With regard to sacrificial offering, livestock, crops, beverages and other articles are given. Giving or offertory in kind would be practical and meaningful for a rural population that has no cash income but has some small production on the farm, rather than for the church to continue extracting money by means of economic compulsion.

## LOCAL BREAD AND WINE

Like eveything else in the development of liturgy, wheat bread and grape wine have been subject to cultural adaptation, as Wainwright writes, 'they are further instances of historical and geographical particularity'.[1]

It would not be a hypothetical suggestion, as some people try to argue, that if Jesus were in Africa he would use African local foods and local wines. I am sure he would. 1 Timothy 4.3-5 says, 'For everything created by God is good and nothing is to be rejected if it is received with thanksgiving; for then it is consecrated by the word of God and prayer'. To refuse to use African food and drink in the eucharistic liturgy, and to deny some people the sacrament, who because of their economic situation cannot afford to import altar wine from Australia and to have baked wheat bread, is to make the principle of incarnational theology foreign and alien to Africans who strongly believe that God incarnate in Jesus Christ came to save them. Some voices from the western world would always insist on the universality of the elements of western wine and bread, so that if a European came to Africa, he/she would know what he/she was taking, but if it were a local bread from millet or maize and wine from palm trees or bananas, etc., he/she would not be sure what was being taken. I do not think that the rural people in Africa who had never seen grapes know what they drink either. It is a matter of faith. Indigenization of eucharistic liturgy will have to consider very seriously the use of local elements.

During the time of Amin in Uganda, when it was difficult to get things for lack of foreign exchange, the House of Bishops of the Church of Uganda allowed the use of banana juice on an experimental basis in some of the dioceses. And people had no problem with it. This should be encouraged in other provinces.

## OTHER RITES AND OCCASIONAL SERVICES

Anglicans in Africa need to develop new liturgical texts, prayers and rites for other occasions: e.g. different liturgies for all the rites of passage like birth, weaning, naming, initiation, marriage, death, burial, post-burial ceremonies (okwabya olumbe—in Luganda, dispersing death), installation of an heir, healing, etc.

There should be special prayers for farmers, hunters, and fishermen, special litanies for planting and harvesting, and healing services. Since the whole is sacramental and that there is nothing physical that is not spiritual, life has to be celebrated in worship in its entirety, everywhere, every time.

And, as Mbiti says, 'wherever the African is, there is his religion; he carries it to the field, where he is sowing seeds or harvesting a new crop, he takes it with him to a beer party, or to attend a funeral ceremony, and if he is educated he takes religion with him to the examination room at school or in the university. If he is a politician he takes it to the house of parliament'.[1]

In view of this spirituality, indigenous liturgy has to adapt to all these different needs of the people. Even the church calendar should include dates of special men and women who have contributed to the spiritual life of the church, diocese and province. Such would assist people to celebrate the events of the mystery of God in Jesus Christ. It would give them a sense of mission.

---

[1] G. Wainwright, *Localization of Liturgy.*
[2] John S. Mbiti, *African Religions and Philosophy,* p.2.

Another area that might need indigenization is marriage. Marriage in African society is not an individual matter. It is a family or clan affair. All ceremonies of betrothal, exchange or bridal wealth, wedding and the rest are important and strengthen the bond of fellowship between two families and clans. The marriage service should involve the community. It is not a father or a brother or a representative who hands over a bride to the groom, but the whole family/clan to the other family/clan. Perhaps a different symbol which shows the value and worth of a wife, like a cow, goat, or an article valuable in the culture, should be exchanged instead of using rings.

Cultural costumes and dress should be used instead of long white dresses and nets which cost a fortune. Many young men put off marriage because they could not afford a western type of wedding, whereas a simple traditional wedding would have been practicable.

Indigenization of liturgy would not be complete without indigenizing liturgical space, furnishings, vessels, etc. All these should reflect African art and design and symbols. Instead of an imported gold and silver chalice and paten, earthenware, or wooden cups, locally made, could equally serve. Local beautiful baskets could be used as plates. Mats could be used as carpets. Each culture has beautiful things that could be used for the glory of God.

There are many things and areas that need indigenization to make liturgy and worship express the African beauty and joy, but the most important thing is that they should not be an end in themselves, but should help people to worship God in his beauty and holiness and glory. They should enable an African to express himself/herself in worship in response to the loving and saving God.

CONCLUSION

Indigenization of liturgy is not an easy thing. There are a lot of risks, problems, and frustrations. People do not easily change their old views to accept new ones, especially when those threaten their identity and security.

A lot of patience, understanding, study and adaptability is needed. So the Anglican Church in the third world, and especially in Africa, should train people in liturgy. Theological colleges in Africa should take the teaching of the liturgy to be a matter of priority and not expect students only to learn the text of the BCP. Joseph V. McCabe has said that responsible cultural adaptation of liturgy requires adequate personnel trained in the history, theology and tradition of the liturgy. This interdisciplinary study should be encouraged in theological colleges because, 'adaptation of liturgy entails various fields of theology, sciences of anthropology, musicology, art, sociology, language, philosophy'.

Having said all that, we need a word of caution to the western world to stop telling the third world how to revise or what to do in indigenizing liturgies. Mbiti has this to say: 'In particular I would appeal to our brethren in and from Europe and America to allow us to make what in your judgment may be termed mistakes: allow us to make a mess of Christianity in our continent just as, if one may put it mildly, you have made a mess of it in Europe and America ... please allow us to say certain things our own way whether we are wrong or not'.[1]

---

[1] John S. Mbiti, *Christian and Traditional Religions in Africa* (1970).

# 7. Ite, Missa Est:
# Liturgy and the Church in Mission

## by Donald Gray

What is the impression conveyed to those from outside the church who, perhaps accidentally, find themselves confronted by the mysteries of Christian worship? We would, of course, wish to deny that there is any 'mystery' about our liturgical practices in the gnostic sense, but I doubt that is the impression gained by the inexperienced visitor. It does seem mysterious and unusual. There are customs, gestures, down-sittings and up-risings that do not seem to have any apparent rationality behind them for those who casually or inquisitively sample our worship. It is too easy for us to forget either the experience of that occasion on which we were first introduced to the customs that now are second nature to us.

Thus it is imperative that we constantly remind ourselves that Christian worship is a 'language' unfamiliar to the majority in our present-day society. How accessible, then, ought we to make it? We might apply a number of tests:

1. Are our 'strange ways' patient of explanation? Have they authentic roots in the history and tradition of Christian worship? Are they capable of exposition in such a way as to deepen and broaden the devotion of both the new and the more experienced worshipper?
2. Of religious ceremonial W. H. Frere asked a question that can be equally applied to the totality of worship. He asked whether our ceremonial patterns are in right analogy with doctrine, and insisted that ceremonies be continually tested for such conformity.[1]
3. Are there customs, ceremonies, words and music that are now merely redolent of a past age, no longer appropriate to present day society? Do they have the effect of making worship merely quaint and antiquarian?
4. How far do our forms of worship create a community that finds it difficult, if not impossible, to be open and receptive to the outsider by encouraging its members to be exclusive and self-regarding? Does our worship contribute to the creation of a missionary-minded congregation or does it merely confirm them in a comfortable feeling of 'club membership' an assurance that the church belongs to 'us' and not to 'them'? The General Synod report, *Faith in the City*, in which the needs of the people in Urban Priority Areas in England are explored, comments:
   'Many Churches convey an attitude of Spirituality which makes prayer and worship available only to those who turn up at the right place at the right time and go through the correct motions from start to finish.'[2]

---

[1] W. H. Frere, *The Principles of Religious Ceremonial* (1906), p.275.
[2] *Faith in the City, A Call for Action by Church and Nation, The Report of the Archbishop's Commission on Urban Priority Areas,* (Church House, London, 1985) 6.105, p.136.